श्री

Jamakkol Prasanam
A Classical Horary System

by

Tirupur S. GopalaKrishnan (GK)

Translated by

Srirangam S. Balaji

INDIA · SINGAPORE · MALAYSIA

Notion Press Media Pvt Ltd

No. 50, Chettiyar Agaram Main Road,
Vanagaram, Chennai, Tamil Nadu – 600 095

First Published by Notion Press 2021
Copyright © Tirupur S. GopalaKrishnan (GK) 2021
All Rights Reserved.

ISBN 978-1-64828-863-0

Index

Introduction

Tiruppur S. Gopalakrishnan (GK)

58 K.N. Building,   98422 20903/20906.
Arisi Kadai street,   gkastro.tirupur@gmail.com
Tiruppur – 4   www.gkastro.org

The astrology is revered as a divine subject. The astrology follows the fundamental rules and the philosophies of the astronomy, the science of space. The astronomical science indicates and locates the position of the planets, the stars and the other heavenly bodies. These are observed entirely by the scientific methods and principles. The subject of astrology recognises these locations and goes beyond these planetary settings. It analyses the effects and influences of those heavenly bodies on the earth and on the human life. There are well established rules and entrusted methods to study those impacts created by the planetary positions and planetary alignments. In the arena of astrology, there are manifold principles and multiple procedures to be followed in casting the horoscopes, fixing the planetary positions, assessing their strengths and finally deriving the predictions by way of analysing the planetary effects and interventions. Many of these rules found their origin in the astronomical data only. But, beyond all the general things of astronomy, the astrology stretches on a higher plane associated with the soul and the intuition. The astrology need not be concomitant to the religion. But it certainly possesses spirulasitic overtones. The astrology can be seen as a complex blend of the information and the intuition. It is the fusion of both the educational and the esoteric philosophies. It is an excellent mix of definitions and the derivations. The astrology is a combination of the scientific principles and the scholarly inferences.

There are various procedures followed in the discipline of astrology to arrive at the predictions. The Prasanam or the Horary system is one of the sure and effective methods of astrological divination. The prasanam in turn has many types and techniques. Here we have chosen to study about the Jamakkol prasanam or the Jamakkol Aarudam. The words Prasanam and Aarudam mean the same thing in this context. The word Jamam or the Yamam refers to the time period of one and half hours or simply 90 minutes. Therefore, a day is filled with 16 Jamam with equal intervals of 90 minutes, eight in the day and another eight in the night. How the planets demonstrate themselves on each and every Jamam for each and every day of the week is the basis of the Jamakkol Prasanam. This is not something contradictory to the conventional astrology. The Jamakkol Prasanam uses all the fundamental principles of the traditional astrology only. The approach is different here. The Jamakkol prasanam is a novel, simple and precise method of prediction.

The Aarudam is the deciding factor in the Jamakkol prasanam. I used to call it in Tamil as, "the Aarudam is the Adhitha palam" which means that the Aarudam is the strongest feature in the determination of the results. And my other quote about the Jamakkol prasanam is," Whenever the question is born, the answer is also born". This means that in the Jamakkol prasanam process any question can be answered. The Udhaya which is equivalent to the ascendant in the natal astrology, the Jama planet in the Udhaya and the Jama graha in the 10th house brings out clearly the mind of the native. The Kavippu, which is a unique determinant in the Jamakkol prasanam method throws light on the hidden things of the query. Once these three things are well understood and fixed properly, the art of prediction becomes not only a cakewalk, but also, the most enjoyable.

I have written six books in Tamil on Jamakkol prasanam starting from the basic learning to the more intense level of the application and usage of the Jamakkol prasanam. If it is about the introduction of the fundamentals of the Jamakkol prasanam and about the case study specimens alone, then, one book is enough. But practicing the Jamakkol prasanam unlocked new and newer insights and amazing experiences. This necessitated the sharing of the new and valuable information and so subsequent volumes of books began to follow. Working on the Jamakkol prasanam has opened innovative challenges and creative possibilities of the Jamakkol system.

For example, we started analysing, why the Sun is exalted when the Guru is in its debilitated state in the Jamakkol planetary arrangement and also vice versa. In astrology, the Mars denotes the men and the Venus represents the women. Why the Mars is exalted when the Venus is debilitated and also vice versa in the Jamakkol Prasanam has to be analysed in this background. Who are the clients we meet when a particular planet is in the Udhaya or in a particular Jamam? Is there any similarity in them or in their problems?

The Udhaya is located on a certain star. Does it bear any significance? If so, what is it? Does the planet approaching the Udhaya dictates the same results related to its Kaaraka all the times or do they differ at certain other times? If yes, why and how they get differentiated. The answers for them lie in the succeeding book, "The advanced techniques in Jamakkol prasanam". That is the subsequent volume of this book to be released very soon. In this present book of basic learning, the identification and the usage of the Aarudam, the Udhayam, the Kavippu, the configuration of Jamakkol planets and the rules for using them are discussed along with case study instances and details. This present book alone will be more than sufficient to provide the needed substance and the stuff to practice the Jamakkol prasanam successfully. We have made our best efforts to condense the 6 books of Tamil into these two capacious volumes for the complete mastery of the Jamakkol system.

I used to cite the real and the original case studies only in my books from my day to day practice of meeting the clients. But, in the astrological consultations, the confidentiality of the customer is essential. Therefore, I give the necessary details only in the case study presentations and the personal information of the clients are either concealed or distorted to preserve their anonymity.

I have to mention about Srirangam Mr. S. Balaji who joined me as a student way back in 2007. Now he has become an integral part of my astrological writings. He has already translated my works like the Chandra Naadi, the Predictions based on transit planets, the Medical astrology and now he has prepared the Jamakkol prasanam text. No doubt it is not an easy job. His fluency over the language of the Tamil and the English combined with his knowledge of astrology has made this challenging task possible and remarkable. To teach about the Jamakkol prasanam in a class room is easy. But to explain it through a book, that too, in English is really a challenge. When I went through the text of this book, I felt greatly satisfied that fair justice has been done to the subject narration. His writing style is lucid and comprehensive and he has presented the book in its full form effectively and interestingly. Mr. S. Balaji has not loaded the book with too much of technical jargons. At the same time, he has not compromised or diluted the core principles of the Jamakkol prasanam. This book will serve both as a text book of learning for the beginners in astrology and as a reference standard for the astrological experts. And, any occasional reader can also find this book informative and fascinating. I bless Mr. S. Balaji good luck and success in all his endeavours.

I request the readers of this book to go through this manuscript gradually and carefully. Being this a new concept, it might take some time to assimilate it. But it is always possible to understand and utilize the Jamakkol prasanam when the basics are learnt. Once you learn the ropes, then you are on your right step towards glory and success in practicing the Jamakkol system. You can share your opinions, doubts, experiences and suggestions with us in updating the book in the future editions. I am happy to share with you that the software application of the Jamakkol prasanam in English is under preparation and anytime from now, it would be made available for the benefit of the astrological community. Again another first from us, and also a feast.

I pray Lord Uchishta Maha Ganapathi to bless us all.

Prologue

Srirangam S. Balaji

84 A Royar Thope.   shreevksharma@gmail.com

Vetri Vinayagar Koil Street.   94438 36104.

Srirangam 620 006.

The venerable science of Astrology deals with the effects and interactions of the planets and the stars on the living beings in the earth. Observation and inference must have been the basis of the evolution of the astrology. The ancient man started to see and spot the strange but regular periodic movements of the celestial bodies. He was the pioneer who laid the foundation stone not only for the astronomy, but also for the astrology. The systematic repetitions of their movements or the placements of the bunch of stars and other cosmic bodies at a fixed place, at a fixed pattern and at a fixed time of the year evoked his curiosity. The other galactic activities like the eclipses, the comets etc., (leave alone the change of seasons, the rain and the storm, the full Moon and new Moon days) induced both fear and also attentiveness on him. When he started to link the heavenly movements with the terrestrial occurrences, or vice versa, the alphabets of the astrology were beginning to take shape. In the primitive period when the primordial man was in search of his food, the shelter and for the safety from natural calamities and wild animals, he took the guidance from the stars for illumination and direction. In due course of time he must have taken those illuminating objects to guide him in his inner life also. This must have paved the path for the evolution for the astrology.

The astrology thus emerged from the observation, the correlation, the imagination, the calculations, the coincidences and finally the recording of these events. The nine planets perpetually revolve around the zodiac squares and locate and relocate themselves at various points of the twenty-seven stars. The resolution is formed in a manifold design of permutations and combinations and thereby they present the kaleidoscope like groupings. This assemblage causes miscellaneous and multiple events and experiences happen in everyone's life. The erudite astrologer deciphers the secrets of these celestial activities using his knowledge of both the astronomy and the astrology. Accordingly, he guides his clients when they approach him. The astrology has thousands of rules and principles. Some of the rules used in astrological texts may look irrelevant, obsolete and may even appear contradictory. But, the scholarly astrologer knows how to use them and where and when. Some people seek the help of the astrologer when they are confused, worried or indecisive. Others pursue the astrologers for clarity and guidance in their endeavours particularly the major ones like the marriage or the business, the health or the litigation. Not only then, but, also to fix the auspicious dates and time for various happenings in their lives, people took the help of the astrologers. The horoscopes also called as natal charts or birth charts serve the purpose of intervention by the astrologer to analyse, predict and to conclude. The horoscope is the schematic representation of the planets at the time of his/her birth. When the horoscope is used for analysis, it is called as the study of natal astrology.

At the same time, there are people who may not have their horoscopes casted. Some may not be aware of the exact date or the time or the place of their births. On such occasions the astrologer uses the methods of the Horary or the Prasanna to answer his clients. There are about 33 types of Prasanna used. In most of the Prasanna methods, a horoscope is prepared at that instant of the query of the client and the planetary positions of that moment are recorded. And the readings are made using this instantaneous chart for the predictions. For natal horoscopy, the chart might have been prepared long back by someone at somewhere. Many a times, the astrologer who now attends the client may not be the one who prepared the horoscope chart. But in Prasanna methods, the astrologer himself personally prepares the chart of that moment and based on that chart, he answers the client who is now sitting before him. When we compare both the Natal and the Prasanna procedures, the natal horoscopy is an overview of the complete life of the client. It covers the entire span of his life. Whereas, the Prasanna system scans the particular portion in the chart which is pertaining to the present-day question and the existing situation. The Prasanna concentrates on that specific aspect of the query and goes deeper into it and took a fine microscopic view. So the answers will be precise and to the point. The prasanam is sharper and straighter. The Prasanna does not touch upon the areas outside the purview of the current question. In Prasanna, it is always instructed that the person concerned must be present before the astrologer for his/her consultation. In addition to the astrological rules, the Prasanna takes into account the various omens and events happening at that time into consideration and imbibes them also into the predictions. In fact, the omens are so powerful, that there could be numerous instances in every astrologers' life, that these omens themselves have professed the accurate results.

In this book the fundamentals, techniques, applications, casting methods, utilities, etc., of the Jamakkol Prasanam are discussed. Simple and suitable examples are given at appropriate places with adequate explanations. The clear understanding of the basic structure is required and it is vital to comprehend and practice the system. The study and the success of the Jamakkol prasanam needs the thorough mastery of the fundamentals. The rules used here are very simple and unique to the Jamakkol prasanam system. They have their basics in the traditional astrology only but the methodology is quite different.

The Jamakkol prasanam is a Prasanna method widely being used in Tamilnadu. The book Sinenthira Malai is a classic work on astrology in Tamil and it is said to be the basis of this system. This technique is based on simple but well distinguished rules. Thiru Kalyanarama Iyer, Alliendhal Thiru. Arunachalam and Jothida

Kadal Trichy Thiru. Vaidhyanatha Iyer were the distinguished pioneers of the Jamakkol system in the yesteryears. They have made valuable contribution to the origin and the formulation of the rules and the structure of the Jamakkol prasanam. But, unfortunately, it seems that it was not widely propagated or practiced in those days. Later, in the recent years, Tiruppur Thiru S. Gopalakrishnan was the man behind the successful revival of the Jamakkol Prasanam. He modified the system in the present easy, simple and user friendly format. He not only wrote books on the subject of Jamakkol Prasanam, but also brought about the first software application for the Jamakkol system. The Jamakkol prasanam software is now available in both the desktop and the Mobile versions.

The Jamakkol software module and his books in Tamil on this topic popularized the system and made it accessible within the comprehensive ability of the astrologers. More and more astrologers started learning this technique from him. They began using it successfully and the system gained immense popularity and wide acceptance. His work on the Jamakkol prasanam were such noteworthy, that his name became synonymous with the Jamakkol system of prasanam. The present Jamakkol prasanam book in the English language is yet another first in the propagation of Jamakkol prasanam method. It is also an addition of one more feather in the cap of Mr. S. Gopalakrishnan in his ongoing yeoman service to the field of astrology in general and the Jamakkol prasanam in particular.

In this book we have made our best efforts to make the readers familiarise and to learn how to apply the Jamakkol prasanam with accuracy, clarity and simplicity. The subject of Jamakkol prasanam is discussed fully and thoroughly. In Tamil, there are six volumes of books on Jamakkol Prasanam written by Tiruppur S. Gopalakrishnan. And almost all of them have come with successful reprints and subsequent editions. In English, it is planned to have two voluminous books. This first volume of the book on the Jamakkol prasanam in English consists of the Fundamentals of the subject meticulously explained from basic concepts, principles, rules, uses and illustrative case studies with sufficient descriptions. The next volume which will be released soon will have the advanced techniques and applications of the Jamakkol prasanam and also more interesting and complicated case studies. We have not limited ourselves in any way and we are ready and willing to share the treasured resources. So it's not the question of a single volume or multiple volumes of book on the subject. It is only on the content and the need on which we are concentrating. Accordingly, we have planned the presentation in a simple, step by step, logical and methodical approach. It will be easy, informative and exact learning even to the unknown reader who is buying and reading this book at somewhere. We welcome the valuable opinions and suggestions for further improvement of this book. Any doubts of the readers can always be cleared through mail correspondence with us.

The success of this book is largely due to the enormous freedom given to me by Tiruppur Thiru S. Gopalakrishnan. He has given me absolute autonomy in my text script. His confidence on me is such, that he has hardly interfered in anything in my writing style, the contents of the subject, the arrangement of the chapters, the selection and the description of the case studies, so on and so forth. Even he has never asked me when the book will be ready. He has simply guided me by his occasional and opt remarks. I took my own time and discretion in perfecting the work assigned to me by him. I have put my finest effort and efficiency to incorporate the essence of the enormous experience and enviable expertise of Thiru GK and brought out this book on the Jamakkol prasanam. I express my sincere gratitude to him and GK Astro academy for entrusting me to carry out this inspiring and pioneering work. It is a great moment to see the astrological wisdom of Thiru GK is crossing the language barriers and is made available to one and all spreading across the boundaries. My pranams and regards to Thiru GK. May his works reach the nook and the corner of the astrological world.

My Namaskarams to my mother Smt. Lalitha Subramanian who has been my support and the spectator of my writing works. I have made all possible efforts to make this Jamakkol Aarudam principles accessible and enlightening to each and every reader. I wish Good luck to all the patrons of this book, who are the ultimate beneficiaries and the judges.

Concept of the Jamakkol Prasanam

The Jamam refers to the time period of one and half hours or 90 minutes. A day of 24 hours is divided in to 16 equal Jamam durations. The day time consist of 8 identical Jamam intervals and the night time another 8 similar Jamam periods. Kol refers to the Tamil word for the Planets or the Grahas. Thus the word Jamakkol refers to the Planet in the Jamam period. The nine planets are made into 8 with the Rahu and the Ketu treated as a single entity. These 8 planets are called as Jamam planets and they are marked outside the zodiac square in this system. The Jamam planets rule each Jamam for one and half hours and then they move in an orderly and in cycle wise fashion. How they are arranged and how they move about and what they reveal by their perpetual movements are discussed in detail in succeeding pages.

The Jamam planets are written outside the zodiac squares. The regular transiting planets are written inside the zodiac squares. The inner or the or transit planets and the outer or the Jamam planets possess all the regular features allotted to the planets. They do not have any kaaraka difference. They differ in their speed and the way in which they move around the zodiac chart. The inner planets can be compared to the roots of a plant and the outer planets to the flowers in the plant. The roots are the real strength for the planets. Similarly, the inner planets decide the strength of the outer planets. For example, when the Guru is at the Kataka in the outer orbit of the zodiac and the transit Guru is in the debilitated state in the Capricorn, then that Guru must be considered as to be in the debilitated state only. The conclusion will be the kaaraka of the Guru looks stronger in the external appearance, but, inwardly it is not so.

Basics of the Jamakkol Prasanam

The following ten factors are very vital in the Jamakkol Prasanam. They must be understood clearly before proceeding. Each of these features are explained in detail with descriptive examples wherever necessary.

1. The Aarudam.

2. The Udhaya lagna simply the Udhayam or the Udhaya.

3. The Veedhi.

4. The Kavippu.

5. The Jamakkol timings.

6. The Jamakkol planetary configuration.

7. The timing of the prasanam.

8. The transit planets

9. The Rasi, the bhava and the planetary kaarakathuvam.

10. The Rasmi or the Rays of the Planets and the Rasis.

The ten parameters listed here seem to be diverse in content and unaccustomed in name, but, actually they are the integral parts of the Jamakkol prasanam. Each of them has a contributory role and a clear significance. The beauty is that both individually and collectively they help to arrive at the conclusions in the astrological predictions. When the names and the methods to find them are familiarised, it comes easy and handy to prepare the Jamakkol charts. Once the charts are successfully erected, the predictions are effortlessly perceptible.

1. The Aarudam

The Aarudam is a time period of 5 minutes. In one hour the Aarudam covers the entire 12 signs.

55 – 60 Meena	00 – 05 Mesha	05 – 10 Rishaba	10 - 15 Mithuna
50 – 55 Kumbha	*Aarudam timings (in minutes) and Rasis*		15 – 20 Kataka
45 – 50 Makara			20 – 25 Simha
40 – 45 Dhanus	35 – 40 Virschika	30 – 35 Thula	25 – 30 Kanya

How the Aarudam is useful in the Jamakkol prasanam? The Aarudam is the most significant factor. With the Aarudam, any question can be attended in the Jamakkol Prasanam. The Aarudam is the valuable contributor to the prediction.

1. The Aarudam tells about the past happenings. The situations and the events that the client had crossed in the past are derived from the Aarudam.

2. The Aarudam indicates the mind of the native. Every person will have many doubts, queries and thoughts in his mind at any point of time, which is natural only. But the Aarudam distinguishes the one most important thing priortising at his mind, which is the prime reason of his present visit to the astrologer. The persuading query is identified by the astrologer using the Aarudam.

3. In the Jamakkol prasanam we use the kaarakathuvam of the planet which is placed in the Udhaya lagna for the predictions.

Every planet has various and variety of kaarakathuvam. The Aarudam is used to identify the kaarakathuvam which is related to the present query. For instance, when the Guru is placed in the Udhaya lagna, it indicates that the customer's purpose of visit is related to the significators of the Guru. But the Guru has listless significators and which one to choose now has to be decided. Now if the Aarudam is in the 2nd bhava from the Udhaya, the Guru indicates the query is related to money. Because the Guru is Dhana Kaaraka. If the Guru is in the fifth bhava it now indicates the child, being it the Puthra kaaraka. Similarly, the Moon indicates the mother in the 4th house and food in the 6th house. The Saturn indicates the longevity when the Aarudam is in the 8th house and the profession when the Aarudam is placed in the 10th. Thus the Aarudam differentiates and helps to determine the exact kaarakathuvam. And thereby the Aarudam supports to recognise the clients' questions among so many options.

In earlier days, the Aarudam was decided from the direction in which the client comes. There might be situations when the client met the astrologer near the river, or paddy fields or even on the road. So the astrologer determined the sign of the Aarudam from the different directions the client approach him. But, nowadays when the astrologer sits in an office and whenever the client comes, they must sit in the chairs in front of him. So it would be almost the same Aarudam always. To overcome this, the minute's wise variation was brought in by Tiruppur S. Gopalakrishnan. His indigenous way of working the Aarudam for the twelve signs from the 12 equal divisions of minutes of an hour was simple. Moreover, it revolutionised and also simplified the system of Jamakkol prasanam and made it within the reach and the understanding of all the astrologers.

The Aarudam is of five minutes' duration. The first Aarudam of the five minutes falls on the Mesha, the next five minutes is in the Rishaba, the third five minutes will be in the Mithuna and it goes on till the Meena rasi. The exact time of the question by the native is noted. Then the hour part in it is deleted and only the minutes are taken for consideration. Say, if it is 14 32 hours, the hour 14 is removed and the minutes 32 is taken for Aarudam calculations. As per the chart, the time 32 represents the Thula rasi. So the Aaruda is written in that sign. It is just that much simple to calculate the Aarudam.

Another example. It is now 06 hours and 24 minutes. Now the number in the hour column is ignored. The digits in the minute's column only are taken. So 24 is our required time now. As per our Aaruda chart, 24 falls in the Simha rasi. So the Aarudam is now marked in the Simha rasi. Hence, in a period of one hour, there will be twelve Aaruda of each five minute's duration. Thus in an approximate period of one hour of Udhaya, there will be twelve Aaruda classifications.

Now, we will take another example. Here a person comes exactly at 15 minutes and so there could be a confusion where to put the Aarudam. Will the Aarudam be in the Mithuna or in the Kataka? In those type of border line situations, the colour of the dress of the client will indicate whether it is the Mithuna or the Kataka. If he is wearing the colours related to the Mithuna or the Bhudha like green shades, the Aarudam is in the Mithuna rasi. But if he wears something in grey or creamy white, the Aarudam is placed in the Kataka rasi. This is applicable to all the rasis where the time is exactly on the border. There is no need to doubt this method of fixing the Aaruda. In the day to day practice, it can be observed that this gives flawless results.

The following chart also explains the correlation of the Rasis and the minutes in fixing the Aarudam. Every Aarudam lasts for a period of five minutes. The time starts at 00 minutes at the Mesha rasi and changes to the next rasi in the succeeding five minute intervals. It ends at the

Meena rasi at the end of the 60 minutes. Then again, it starts its cycle from the Mesha rasi.

Serial number	Minutes	Aarudam
01	00 – 05	Mesha
02	05 – 10	Rishaba
03	10 – 15	Mithuna
04	15 – 20	Kataka
05	20 – 25	Simha
06	25 – 30	Kanya
07	30 – 35	Thula
08	35 – 40	Virschika
09	40 – 45	Dhanus
10	45 – 50	Makara
11	50 – 55	Kumbha
12	55 – 60	Meena

2. The Udhayam

The Udhayam in the Jamakkol Prasanam is equivalent to the Ascendant used in the natal horoscopy. This is also called as the Udhaya lagna and its lord as the Udhaya adhipathi. The Udhaya is used to study the predictions about the future. The Udhaya plays the pivotal role in answering the queries of the client. Anything and everything can be inferred from the Udhaya. The Udhaya is a time period of approximately one hour, but it varies between 56 minutes to 64 minutes. There are 12 Udhaya lagna in the day time and another 12 Udhaya lagna in the night time. One Udhaya covers the span of one Rasi in the zodiac.

The Udhaya is calculated by the Jamakkol software applications nowadays. But it is always suggested to learn how to calculate it manually also. There are various methods used to calculate the Udhaya. Here we present the two simple common methods.

To calculate the Udhaya we need to know the timing of the Sun rise and the Sun set and also the degree wise position of the transit Sun on that day of the Prasanam.

Method 1

The time of the Sunrise is subtracted from the time of the query (means the time of the analysis).

The time of the query   10 h 21 minutes

The time of the Sunrise   06 h 06 minutes

Subtracting..........   04 h 15 minutes

Converting this into minutes, (4 × 60) + 15 = 255 minutes.

To change this into degrees, we have to divide it by 2.

So.......................   255/2 = 127 degrees and 30 minutes.

Now add this with the degree of the transit Sun 111 degrees and 18 minutes.

(This is the position of the Sun on 08/08/2019)

Adding ....   238 degrees and 48 minutes.

This degree falls in the sign of Scorpio in the star Jyeshta 3rd pada in the zodiac circle.

So the Scorpio is the Udhaya and the Jyeshta the Udhaya nakshtra and the Mars the Udhaya adhipathi. If the Udhaya lagna degree crosses 360, subtract 360 from the value and then fix the Udhaya lagna.

Duration of the each Udhaya is calculated from the timings of Sun rise and Sunset of that place where the astrologer does his calculations. The time and place of the query is always based on the location of the astrologer and never on the querist.

The time period between one Sun rise and the next Sun set is called as Ahas and the time between one Sun set to the next Sun rise is called as Rathra and both put together contribute to a Ahorathra (one full day of 24 hours).

The Sun set on 08/08/2019   18 h 33 m

The Sunrise of 08/08/2019   06 h 06 m

Subtracting……….   12 h 27 m

Converting this into minutes, $(12 \times 60) + 27 = 747$ minutes.

This is for the period of 12 hours of Ahas period. There are 12 Udhaya lagna in that particular period. So the duration of 12 Udhaya is equal to 747 minutes.

Therefore, the duration of one Udhaya is equal to $747/12 = 62. 25$ or rounded off to 62 minutes.

This is the duration of one Udhaya.

To find the Udhayam

Method 2

The Udhayam or the Udhaya lagna is the rising sign at the time of the query to the astrologer. The Udhayam used in the prasanam is equivalent to the Lagna in the natal chart. There are 12 lagna in a period of 24 hours each measuring approximately 2 hours in the natal horoscopy. Likewise, there are 12 Udhaya lagna for the day time and twelve Udhaya lagna for the night in the Jamakkol prasanam. The duration of the Udhaya lagna is roughly 1 hour. The duration of the Udhaya varies between 56 minutes to 64 minutes.

The basis of calculation to find out the Udhayam is given here. For this we need the time of Sun rise and the Sun set at that place and the date according to the Tamil calendar (according to the Solar month system).

Let 06 06 am is the time of Sun rise and 17 46 hours be the time of Sun set. Now we have to find the daytime duration. For that we have *to subtract the Sun rise time from the Sun set time.*

Sun set	*17 46 hours*
Sun rise	*06 06 hours*
Subtraction	*1 40 hours*

Converting the hours into minutes, (11 X 60) + 40 = (660 + 40) = 700 minutes.

This is the duration of the day time called Ahas. The Udhayam travels the 12 signs of the Zodiac once in a day and once in the night time. So dividing 700 minutes by 12 to calculate time period of the Udhaya for the day time.

700/12 = 58. 3 minutes or 58 minutes. This is the duration of one Udhaya lagna for the day.

From the time of the Sun rise the first Udhaya lagna will be in vogue for 58 minutes. This first udhaya will be incidentally the same sign in which the Sun is transiting at that particular time. The next Udhaya lagna will commence only after the next 58 minutes. We can now find out how Udhaya lagna is calculated with an example.

Date 27/06/2019. (Equivalent Solar month day Mithuna [Aani 12])

Place. Srirangam, Tiruchirappalli.	Time 11 52 hrs.
Sun rise:	06 03 am
Sun set:	06 36 pm or 18 36 hours

Let us Subtract the 06 03 from 18 36. We get 12 hours and 33 minutes. Converting it to minutes, (12 × 60) + 33 = 720 + 33 = 753 minutes.

This is the duration of the day, also called as the Ahas time. Now dividing it among 12 Udhaya periods, 753 /12 = 62. 09 minutes or 63 minutes (approximately).

The first Mithuna Udhaya will start at the Sun rise time and will prevail for the 63 minutes.

Twelve days have already passed in the month of the Mithuna. The Sun travels 4 minutes of in a day or approximately one degree per day in the 360-degree zodiac. The Sun travels 2 minutes in the day time and 2 in the night time. In 12 days of Mithuna month, the Sun must have crossed 24 minutes from the Sun rise time. So this 24 minutes has to be subtracted from the Udhaya time of 63 minutes. (63 – 24 = 39 minutes). This 39 minutes is the balance of time which the transit Sun will be in the Mithuna Udhaya. Therefore, the first Udhaya of the Mithuna will be in vogue for 39 minutes after the Sun rise.

Sun rise time	06 03 h min
Duration of Mithuna Udhaya	00 39 h min
Adding	06 42 h min

This is the time in which the Mithuna Udhaya gets completed and the next Udhaya of Kataka begins here.

Commencement of Kataka Udhaya	06 42
Duration of one Udhaya lagna	00 63 minutes.
Adding	07 45 Kataka Udhaya completed.
Adding once again Udhaya duration	00 63 minutes.
	08 48 Simha Udhaya completed.
Adding again one Udhaya duration	00 63 minutes.
	09 51 Kanya Udhaya completed.
Adding again one Udhaya duration	00 63 minutes.
	10 54 Thula Udhaya completed.

Adding again one Udhaya duration	00 63 minutes.
	11 57 Virschika Udhaya completed.
Adding again one Udhaya duration	00 63 minutes.
	13 00 Dhanus Udhaya completed.
Adding again one Udhaya duration	00 63 minutes.
	14 03 Makara Udhaya completed.
Adding again one Udhaya duration	00 63 minutes.
	15 06 Kumbha Udhaya completed.
Adding again one Udhaya duration	00 63 minutes.
	16 09 Meena Udhaya completed.
Adding again one Udhaya duration	00 63 minutes.
	17 12 Mesha Udhaya completed.
Adding again one Udhaya duration	00 63 minutes.
	18 15 Rishaba Udhaya completed.

This is how the twelve Udhaya lagna are calculated from the starting of the day at the Mithuna Udhaya lagna. After the time 18 15, the Jamakkol Udhaya timings for the night time start at the same Mithuna and proceed in the same way.

To calculate the duration of each Udhaya for the night duration we have to subtract the Sun set time from the next Sun rise time. In this example the sun set time is 06 36 pm. The next sun rise time for the next day i.e., on 28/06/2019 is 06 04 am. For calculation purposes only, take this as 18 04 and subtract the previous days' sun set time from this.

Sun rise time of 28/06/2019 is 06 04.

Adding 12 to it for mathematical calculation 18 04

Sunset time on 27/06/2019 06 36

Subtracting 11 28

Converting this in to minutes,

$(11 \times 60) + 28 = 688$ minutes.

Divide this by 12, 688/12 = 57. 03 minutes or 57 (approximately).

This is the duration of one Udhaya in the night time and it will start from the Mithuna Rasi only.

(The Udhaya lagna time for the day and the night will be complimentary to each other. If one is 63 the other will be 57. If it is 59, the other will be 61 only)

3. The Veedhi

The position of the transit Sun is taken as the basis for the calculation of the Veedhi. The term Veedhi means the Path. So the Veedhi refers to the track in which the transit Sun is travelling. The Veedhi is classified as the Dhakshnayana, the Uthrayana and the Poorvayana. The months of the Rishaba, the Mithuna, the Kataka and the Leo denotes the Mesha Veedhi. The months of the Meena, the Mesha, the Kanya and the Thula indicates the Rishaba Veedhi. The Virschika, the Dhanus, the Makara and the Kumbha represents the Mithuna Veedhi. When the Sun transits in their respective signs means that the Sun is travelling in that corresponding Veedhi. For instance, if the transit Sun is in the Simha rasi, that means it is passing through the Mesha Veedhi. Similarly, for the other signs. The pictorial representation of the Veedhi and the equivalent rasi is given here.

Rishaba Veedhi	Rishaba Veedhi	Mesha Veedhi	Mesha Veedhi
Mithuna Veedhi	The movements of the transit Sun and the respective Veedhi		Mesha Veedhi
Mithuna Veedhi			Mesha Veedhi
Mithuna Veedhi	Mithuna Veedhi	Rishaba Veedhi	Rishaba Veedhi

The Veedhi is useful to find out the Kavippu.

4. The Kavippu

The Kavippu is another indicator in the Jamakkol prasanam for prediction. The Kavippu is equivalent to the Chatra rasi referred in the classical astrological text Prasanna marga. The nearest equivalent of Kavippu is the Chatra rasi. The Chatra means an umbrella. Like the umbrella the Kavippu hides the secrets of the Prasanam. The umbrella is like a protective covering. Similarly, the Kavippu denotes the hidden things. The loss, the secrets, the depletions of the native are indicated by the Kavippu. The Kavippu will show whether a particular thing will happen or not. The position of the Kavippu is dependent on the position of the transit Sun and the Aaruda rasi.

Usually in the astrological consultations, the native tells the astrologer his objective of the visit or he puts his query straight to the astrologer. In some cases, the native expects the astrologer to identify the purpose of his visit by the astrologer himself and so keeps quiet. *In Jamakkol prasanam, when the question is asked direct, the Kavippu indicates the answer. If the question is not asked, the Kavippu indicates the hidden question.* This is the uniqueness and the power of the Kavippu. The Kavippu is a time duration of five minutes. It travels in the anti-clock wise direction in the zodiac.

The calculation to find out Kavippu.

Now find out in which Veedhi the Sun is transiting at the moment of the query. If it is Mesha Veedhi count from the sign of the Aarudam up to Mesha rasi. If it is in the Rishaba Veedhi, count from the Aarudam to the Rishaba sign. When it is in the Mithuna Veedhi, count from the Aarudam up to the Mithuna rasi. Let X be the number of signs from the Aarudam to Mesha or Rishaba or Mithuna rasi. In all these situations, now count the same number X from the sign of Udhaya lagna and put the Kavippu in that sign. This is how Kavippu is calculated.

Example 1

Udhayam: Simha. Aaruda: Scorpio. Transit Sun: Rishaba.

The transit Sun is at Rishaba means it is Mesha Veedhi. So we have to calculate from Aaruda up to the Mesha rasi. The Mesha veedhi means we have to calculate up to the Mesha rasi. The Rishaba veedhi means we have to count up to the Rishaba rasi. For the Mithuna veedhi, the counting must be done up to the Mithuna rasi. And then calculate the same from the Udhaya and put the Kavippu in that sign. Now in this case, the Aaruda to the Mesha rasi is six signs. So six signs from the Udhaya is the Makara which is the sign of the Kavippu.

	Veedhi	Transit Sun	
Kavippu			Udhaya
	Aaruda		

Example 2

Udhaya: Simha. Aaruda: Scorpio. Transit Sun: Kanya.

The transit Sun at Kanya means it is the Rishaba Veedhi. So we have to calculate from the Aaruda up to the sign Rishaba. And then calculate the same from the Udhaya and put the Kavippu in that sign. There are 7 signs between the Aaruda and the Rishaba rasi. So the Kumbha which is the 7th sign from the Udhaya becomes the place for the Kavippu.

		Veedhi	
Kavippu			
			Udhaya
	Aaruda		Transit Sun

Example 3

Udhaya: Simha. Aaruda: Scorpio. Transit Sun: Makara.

When the transit Sun is in the Makara, the Veedhi is the Mithuna veedhi. So we have to calculate from the Aaruda up to the sign of Mithuna and count the same number from the Udhaya and put the Kavippu there. The signs counted from the Aaruda up to the Mithuna rasi is 8. So when we count 8 from the Simha rasi, the Meena rasi becomes the location of the Kavippu.

Kavippu			Veedhi
Transit Sun			Udhaya
	Aaruda		

The ready reckoner tables are being provided here to calculate the Kavippu for all the three Veedhi patterns. Accordingly, three different tables for the respective Veedhi with the corresponding Udhaya and the Aaruda are given. These tables indicate the position of the Kavippu for all the twelve Udhaya and twelve Aaruda combinations.

TABULAR COLUMN FOR KAVIPPU FOR THE MONTHS OF
RISHABA, MITHUNA, KATAKA, SIMHA

MESHA VEEDHI

	MESHA	RISHABA	MITHUANA	KATAKA	SIMHA	KANYA	THULA	VIRSHKA	DHANUS	MAKARA	KUMBHA	MEENA
						UDHAYA LAGNA						
MESHA	MESHA	RISHABA	METHUNA	KAATAKA	SIMHA	KANYA	THULA	VIRSHIKA	DHANUS	MAKARA	KUMBHA	MEENA
RISHABA	MEENA	MESHA	RISHABA	MITHUNA	KATAKA	SIMHA	KANYA	THULA	VIRSHIKA	DHANUS	MAKARA	KUMBHA
MITHUNA	KUMBHA	MEENA	MESHA	RISHABA	MITHUNA	KATAKA	SIMHA	KANYA	THULA	VIRSHIKA	DHANUS	MAKARA
KATAKA	MAKARA	KUMBHA	MEENA	MESHA	RISHABA	MITHUNA	KATAKA	SIMHA	*KANYA*	THULA	VIRSHIKA	DHANUS
SIMHA	DHANUS	MAKARA	KUMBHA	MEENA	MESHA	RISHABA	MITHUNA	KATAKA	SIMHA	KANYA	THULA	VIRSHIKA
KANYA	VIRSHIKA	DHANUS	MAKARA	KUMBHA	MEENA	MESHA	RISHABA	MITHUNA	KATAKA	SIMHA	KANYA	THULA
THULA	THULA	VIRSHIKA	DHANUS	MAKARA	KUMBHA	MEENA	MESHA	RISHABA	MITHUNA	KATAKA	SIMHA	KANYA
VIRSHIKA	KANYA	THULA	VIRSHIKA	DHANUS	MAKARA	KUMBHA	MEENA	MESHA	RISHABA	MITHUNA	KATAKA	SIMHA
DHANUS	SIMHA	KANYA	THULA	VIRSHIKA	DHANUS	MAKARA	KUMBHA	MEENA	MESHA	RISHABA	MITHUNA	KATAKA
MAKARA	KATAKA	SIMHA	KANYA	THULA	VIRSHIKA	DHANUS	MAKARA	KUMBHA	MEENA	MESHA	RISHABA	MITHUNA
KUMBHA	MITHUNA	KATAKA	SIMHA	KANYA	THULA	VIRSHIKA	DHANUS	MAKARA	KUMBHA	MEENA	MESHA	RISHABA
MEENA	RISHABA	MITHUNA	KATAKA	SIMHA	KANYA	THULA	VIRSHIKA	DHANUS	MAKARA	KUMBHA	MEENA	MESHA

Example: If Aarduam = Kataka, Udhaya → Dhanus then Kavippu → Kanya

TABULAR COLUMN FOR KAVIPPU FOR THE MONTHS OF
MEENA, MESHA, KANYA AND THULA

RISHABA VEEDHI

	UDHAYA LAGNA											
	MESHA	RISHABA	MITHUNA	KATAKA	SIMHA	KANYA	THULA	VIRSHKA	DHANUS	MAKARA	KUMBHA	MEENA
MESHA	RISHABA	MITHUNA	KATAKA	SIMHA	KANYA	THULA	VIRSHIKA	DHANUS	MAKARA	KUMBHA	MEENA	MESHA
RISHABA	MESHA	RISHABA	MITHUNA	KATAKA	SIMHA	KANYA	THULA	VIRSHIKA	DHANUS	MAKARA	KUMBHA	MEENA
MITHUNA	MEENA	MESHA	RISHABA	MITHUNA	KATAKA	SIMHA	KANYA	THULA	VIRSHIKA	DHANUS	MAKARA	KUMBHA
KATAKA	KUMBHA	MEENA	MESHA	RISHABA	MITHUNA	KATAKA	SIMHA	KANYA	THULA	VIRSHIKA	DHANUS	MAKARA
SIMHA	MAKARA	KUMBHA	MEENA	MESHA	RISHABA	MITHUNA	KATAKA	SIMHA	KANYA	THULA	VIRSHIKA	DHANUS
KANYA	DHANUS	MAKARA	KUMBHA	MEENA	MESHA	RISHABA	MITHUNA	KATAKA	SIMHA	KANYA	THULA	VIRSHIKA
THULA	VIRSHIKA	DHANUS	MAKARA	KUMBHA	MEENA	MESHA	RISHABA	MITHUNA	KATAKA	SIMHA	KANYA	THULA
VIRSHIKA	THULA	VIRSHIKA	DHANUS	MAKARA	KUMBHA	MEENA	MESHA	RISHABA	MITHUNA	KATAKA	SIMHA	KANYA
DHANUS	KANYA	THULA	VIRSHIKA	DHANUS	MAKARA	KUMBHA	MEENA	MESHA	RISHABA	MITHUNA	KATAKA	SIMHA
MAKARA	SIMHA	KANYA	THULA	VIRSHIKA	DHANUS	MAKARA	KUMBHA	MEENA	MESHA	RISHABA	MITHUNA	KATAKA
KUMBHA	KATAKA	SIMHA	KANYA	THULA	VIRSHIKA	DHANUS	MAKARA	KUMBHA	MEENA	MESHA	RISHABA	MITHUNA
MEENA	MITHUNA	KATAKA	SIMHA	KANYA	THULA	VIRSHIKA	DHANUS	MAKARA	KUMBHA	MEENA	MESHA	RISHABA

Example : If Aarudham → Kanya, Udhaya → Simhan then Kavippu → Mesha

TABULAR COLUMN FOR KAVIPPU FOR THE MONTHS OF
VIRSHKA, DHANUS, MAKARA, KUMBHAM

MITHUNA VEEDHI

↑	MESHA	RISHABA	MITHUANA	KATAKA	SIMHA	KANYA	THULA	VIRSHKA	DHANUS	MAKARA	KUMBHA	MEENA
						UDHAYA LAGNA						
MESHA	MITHUNA	KATAKA	SIMHA	KANYA	THULA	VIRSHIKA	DHANUS	MAKARA	KUMBHA	MEENA	MESHA	RISHABA
RISHABA	RISHABA	MITHUNA	KATAKA	SIMHA	KANYA	THULA	VIRSHIKA	DHANUS	MAKARA	KUMBHA	MEENA	MESHA
MITHUNA	MESHA	RISHABA	MITHUNA	KATAKA	SIMHA	KANYA	THULA	VIRSHIKA	DHANUS	MAKARA	KUMBHA	MEENA
KATAKA	MEENA	MESHA	RISHABA	MITHUNA	KATAKA	SIMHA	KANYA	THULA	VIRSHIKA	DHANUS	MAKARA	KUMBHA
SIMHA	KUMBHA	MEENA	MESHA	RISHABA	MITHUNA	KATAKA	SIMHA	KANYA	THULA	VIRSHIKA	DHANUS	MAKARA
KANYA	MAKARA	KUMBHA	MEENA	MESHA	RISHABA	MITHUNA	KATAKA	SIMHA	KANYA	THULA	VIRSHIKA	DHANUS
THULA	DHANUS	MAKARA	KUMBHA	MEENA	MESHA	RISHABA	MITHUNA	KATAKA	SIMHA	KANYA	THULA	VIRSHIKA
VIRSHIKA	VIRSHIKA	DHANUS	MAKARA	KUMBHA	MEENA	MESHA	RISHABA	MITHUNA	KATAKA	SIMHA	KANYA	THULA
DHANUS	THULA	VIRSHIKA	DHANUS	MAKARA	KUMBHA	MEENA	MESHA	RISHABA	MITHUNA	KATAKA	SIMHA	KANYA
MAKARA	KANYA	THULA	VIRSHIKA	DHANUS	MAKARA	KUMBHA	MEENA	MESHA	RISHABA	MITHUNA	KATAKA	SIMHA
KUMBHA	SIMHA	KANYA	THULA	VIRSHIKA	DHANUS	MAKARA	KUMBHA	MEENA	MESHA	RISHABA	MITHUNA	KATAKA
MEENA	KATAKA	SIMHA	KANYA	THULA	VIRSHIKA	DHANUS	MAKARA	KUMBHA	MEENA	MESHA	RISHABA	MITHUNA

Example :: If Aarduam → Meena, Udhayam → Dhanus, Then Kavippu → Meena

5. Jamakkol Timings

As we have seen, the Jamam is a period of 90 minutes. And the total duration of the eight Jamam took 720 minutes or 12 hours. This is the period of a day time. Another 12 hours constitute the night time, putting the total period of the 8 plus 8 Jamam in a full day of 24 hours. The Jamam timings both in the day and in the night start at the Meena rasi and move around the zodiac in an anticlockwise direction. While doing so they cover the Movable and the Common signs and skip the Fixed signs. This never meant that they jump those rasis. In fact, the first fifteen degrees of the Fixed sign will act like the Movable sign proceeding it. The next fifteen degrees resemble the character of the Common sign which follows it. So a Jamam covers 45 degrees in a period of its duration of 90 minutes. It takes two minutes to cover one degree of the zodiac. The Jamakkol timings of the rasis are always constant for all the weekdays and they never change. The planetary positions only will change as per the day of the week.

06 00 – 07 30	04 30 – 06 00	X	03 00 – 04 30
X	*Jamam timings {Common for both the day and the night}*		01 30 – 03 00
07 30 – 09 00			X
09 00 – 10 30	X	10 30 – 12 00	12 00 – 01 30

In this timing pattern we don't use the Fixed signs (Sthira rasis). That's why we have marked X in those four squares, the Rishaba, the Simha, the Virschika and the Kumbha.

The Jama Grahas are not mentioned in the Sthira rasis, but, they travel via them only from the Common signs to the Movable signs. Therefore, the degree wise position or the nakshtra pada wise arrangement is mentioned for all the Jama Grahas in the Fixed signs also.

6. Configuration of Jamakkol Planets

In Jamakkol prasanam we use the Jamakkol planets which are put outside the zodiac chart. It is a unique arrangement of the planets. The day as well as the night is divided into eight equal parts, each measuring one and a half hour. So totally 8 plus 8 divisions share this 24 hours' time period. This one-and-a-half-hour period is called a Jamam. Thus Jamam is a period of 90 minutes' duration. Each Jamam division is ruled by a planet and thus all the eight planets rule the eight divisions of Jamam. The planets in the transit are put inside the zodiac squares. The eight Jamakkol planets are placed outside the zodiac square nearer to the signs they rule in the respective Jamam. The procedure of the planets in the Jamakkol system starts from the Sun, the Mars, the Jupiter, the Mercury, the Venus, the Moon, the Saturn and the Snake. Here both the Rahu and the Ketu are combined in one common name **the Snake.** These eight planets are used against the four Movable and the Four Common signs. The Fixed signs are not considered here.

The lord of the day of the Prasanam starts first at the Meena rasi in the first Jama duration of the time starting from 6 o'clock. The first Jamam prevails for the period of 90 minutes or one and half an hour time period. The other seven Jamakkol planets fill up their respective places as per their sequential arrangement. Now at 7 30 the day lord moves from the Meena to the next square Makara and the other planets follow the suit. This is the second Jamam of the day. The day lord can be compared to a railway engine which pulls the other seven compartments as it moves from one square to the next in its transit in the Jamam timings. The 8 Jamam timings in the day follow in this same order. Now follows the cycle of planets in the night Jamam timings. It is the same order as happened in the day time, once again the day lord leading the array of planets as before starting from the Meena rasi and travelling in the anti-clockwise direction. The arrangement of the planets in the eight different Jamam are tabulated here for quick reference.

The planet which appears in the Meena rasi in the first Jamam of the day is the day lord of that particular day. For example, on Thursdays, the Guru occupies the Meena rasi in the first Jama timing of 06 to 07 30. So that is the day lord. The Guru acts like a leader on that day and rules all the other planets under its influence. This is true for all the other planets also. They rule the rest of the planets on their respective day when they become the day lord.

Jamam	1	2	3	4	5	6	7	8
Timings	6 00 to 7 30	7 30 to 9 00	9 00 to 10 30	10 30 to 12 00	1200 to 1 30	13 30 to 15 00	15 00 to 16 30	16 30 to18 00
Day/Signs	Pisces	Capricorn	Sagittarius	Libra	Virgo	Cancer	Gemini	Aries
Sunday	Sun	Mars	Jupiter	Mercury	Venus	Saturn	Moon	Snake
Monday	Moon	Snake	Sun	Mars	Jupiter	Mercury	Venus	Saturn
Tuesday	Mars	Jupiter	Mercury	Venus	Saturn	Moon	Snake	Sun
Wednesday	Mercury	Venus	Saturn	Moon	Snake	Sun	Mars	Jupiter
Thursday	Jupiter	Mercury	Venus	Saturn	Moon	Snake	Sun	Mars
Friday	Venus	Saturn	Moon	Snake	Sun	Mars	Jupiter	Mercury
Saturday	Saturn	Moon	Snake	Sun	Mars	Jupiter	Mercury	Venus

The arrangements of the Jamakkol planets is shown here in the form of the horoscope charts. This is the example of the chart for the first Jamam of Thursday. The time for the first Jamam is 6 00 to 7 30. This time is the same for the first Jamam both in the day and in the night. The day lord Jupiter is placed in the Meena rasi. The rest of the planets are arranged as per the Jamakkol sequential arrangement of the planets. The Jamakkol structure starts from the Meena rasi and travel in the anticlock wise direction around the Zodiac and finally ends up at the Mesha rasi. Again, for the night time it starts from the Meena rasi as before and reaches the Mesha rasi travelling along the zodiac during the 8 Jamam intervals.

Jupiter	Mars		Sun
06 00 to 7 30	04 30 to 06 00		03 00 to 04 30
			01 30 to 03 00 — Snake
Mercury — 07 30 to 09 00			
09 00 to 10 30		1030 to 1200	12 00 to 01 30
Venus		Saturn	Moon

In this Jamam the Mars and the Jupiter occupy their own houses and the Saturn is in its exalted state. The Rahu kaal timing of Thursday is from 3 pm to 4 30 pm. In the chart we can find that the Snake is present in that time slot which is in Kataka. It is instructed to always bear in mind that during the first Jamam of the day, the Snake will occupy the slot of the Rahu kaal timing of that particular day. This is a useful tip to check whether the Jamam planets are written correctly. This tip is true for the first Jamam of the day only.

Serial Number	Day	Rahukaal time	Jamam	Snake location
1	Sunday	04 30-06 00 p.m.	Eighth	Mesha
2	Monday	07 30-09 00 a.m.	Second	Makara
3	Tuesday	03 00-04 30 p.m.	Seventh	Mithuna
4	Wednesday	12noon-130p.m.	Fifth	Kanya
5	Thursday	0130-03 00 p.m.	Sixth	Kataka
6	Friday	1030a.m-12noon	Fourth	Thula
7	Saturday	09 00-10 30 a.m.	Third	Dhanus

In the arrangement of the Jamakkol planets, the Sun and the Venus will always be opposite to each other. The Moon will be positioned opposite to the Jupiter. The Mercury and the Snake will be located against each other. The Saturn and the Mars will be face to face to each other. This arrangement of planets is permanent. If we remember this sequential construction, we can check whether we have put the Jamam planets in the proper order.

The arrangement of the eight Jamam intervals and the corresponding time of each Jamam and the position of them in the respective rasis is tabulated here.

Serial number	Jamam	Time (day/night)	Rasi
1	First	06 00 - 07 30	Meena/Pisces
2	Second	07 30 - 09 00	Makara/Capricorn
3	Third	09 00 - 10 30	Dhanus/Sagittarius
4	Fourth	10 30 - 12 00	Thula/Libra
5	Fifth	12 00 - 01 30	Kanya/Virgo
6	Sixth	01 30 - 03 00	Kataka/Cancer
7	Seventh	03 00 - 04 30	Mithuna/Gemini
8	Eighth	04 30 - 06 00	Mesha/Aries

The Jamakkol planetary arrangements for all the seven days covering the entire 8 Jamam timings are illustrated here. The Jamam timings for the day are 8 and for the night are 8 and thus totally there are 16 Jamams in a day of 24 hours. But for the same Jamam of one and half an hour, the planetary configuration is same both in the day and the night. If the Sun is in the Meena rasi in the first Jamam of the day of the time between 06 00 a.m. to 07 30 a.m., then the Sun will be in the same Meena rasi in the first Jamam of the night which is the time between 06 00 p.m. to 07 30 p.m.

Here the 8 Jamam arrangements of the day (as well as the night) for the 7 weekdays are given. These total 56 charts will serve as a ready reckoner for the Jamakkol chart preparation.

Sunday

The first Jamam both in the day and the night will always have the day's lord in the Meena rasi and the other planets follow the sequential arrangement in the anti-clockwise manner. The planetary position will be the same in the day and the night for any particular time.

1. Time of the first Jamam in the day and night. 06 00 to 07 30. Both day and night.

Sun		Snake			Moon
	06 00 to 07 30	04 30 to 06 00		03 00 to 04 30	
				01 30 to 03 00	Sat
Mars	07 30 to 09 00				
	09 00 to 10 30		1030 to 1200	12 00 to 01 30	
Jupiter			Mercury		Venus

2. Sunday. The second Jamam. Time. 07 30 to 9 00. Both day and night.

Snake	Moon		Saturn
06 00 to 07 30	04 30 to 06 00		03 00 to 04 30
		01 30 to 03 00	Venus
Sun 07 30 to 09 00			
09 00 to 10 30	10 30 to 12 00		12 00 to 01 30
Mars		Jupiter	Mercury

1. **Sunday. The third Jamam. Time 9 00 to 10 30. Both day and night.**

Moon	Saturn		Venus
06 00 to 07 30	04 30 to 06 00		03 00 to 04 30
			01 30 to 03 00 — Mercury
Snake — 07 30 to 09 00			
09 00 to 10 30		10 30 to 12 00	12 00 to 01 30
Sun		Mars	Jupiter

2. Sunday. The fourth Jamam of Sunday. Time 10 30 to 12 00. Both day and night.

Saturn		Venus		Mercury
	06 00 to 07 30	04 30 to 06 00		03 00 to 04 30
				01 30 to 03 00 — Jupiter
Moon	07 30 to 09 00			
	09 00 to 10 30		10 30 to 12 00	12 00 to 01 30
Snake		Sun		Mars

3. The fifth Jamam of Sunday. Time 12 00 to 01 30. Both day and night.

Venus		Mercury			Jupiter
	06 00 to 07 30	04 30 to 06 00		03 00 to 04 30	
				01 30 to 03 00	Mars
Saturn	07 30 to 09 00				
	09 00 to 10 30		10 30 to 12 00	12 00 to 01 30	
Moon			Snake		Sun

4. The Sixth Jamam of Sunday. Time 01 30 to 03 00. Both day and night.

Mercury	Jupiter		Mars
06 00 to 07 30	04 30 to 06 00		03 00 to 04 30
			01 30 to 03 00 — Sun
Venus — 07 30 to 09 00			
09 00 to 10 30		10 30 to 12 00	12 00 to 01 30
Saturn		Moon	Snake

5. **The Seventh Jamam of Sunday. Time. 03 00 to 04 30. Both day and night.**

Jupiter		Mars			Sun
	06 00 to 07 30	04 30 to 06 00		03 00 to 04 30	
				01 30 to 03 00	Snake
Mercury	07 30 to 09 00				
	09 00 to 10 30		10 30 to 12 00	12 00 to 01 30	
Venus			Saturn		Moon

6. The Eighth Jamam of Sunday. Time. 04 30 to 06 00. Both day and night.

Mars	Sun		Snake
06 00 to 07 30	04 30 to 06 00	03 00 to 04 30	
		01 30 to 03 00	Moon
Jupiter — 07 30 to 09 00			
09 00 to 10 30	10 30 to 12 00	12 00 to 01 30	
Mercury	Venus		Saturn

1. **Monday. The first Jamam. Time 06 to 07 30. Both day and night.**

Moon	Saturn		Venus
06 00 to 07 30	04 30 to 06 00		03 00 to 04 30
			01 30 to 03 00 / Mercury
Snake / 07 30 to 09 00			
09 00 to 10 30		10 30 to 12 00	12 00 to 01 30
Sun		Mars	Jupiter

2. Monday. The second Jamam. Time 07 30 to 09 00. Both day and night.

Saturn	Venus		Mercury
06 00 to 07 30	04 30 to 06 00		03 00 to 04 30
			01 30 to 03 00 — Jupiter
Moon — 07 30 to 09 00			
09 00 to 10 30		10 30 to 12 00	12 00 to 01 30
Snake		Sun	Mars

7. **Monday. The 3rd Jamam. Time 09 00 to 10 30. Both day and the night.**

Venus		Mercury			Jupiter
	06 00 to 07 30	04 30 to 06 00		03 00 to 04 30	
				01 30 to 03 00	Mars
Saturn	07 30 to 09 00				
	09 00 to 10 30		10 30 to 12 00	12 00 to 01 30	
Moon			Snake		Sun

4. Monday. The 4th Jamam. Time 10 30 to 12 00. Both day and night.

Mercury		Jupiter			Mars
	06 00 to 07 30	04 30 to 06 00		03 00 to 04 30	
				01 30 to 03 00	Sun
Venus	07 30 to 09 00				
	09 00 to 10 30		10 30 to 12 00	12 00 to 01 30	
Saturn			Moon		Snake

5. Monday. The 5ᵗʰ Jamam. Time. 12 00 to 01 30. Both day and night.

Jupiter	Mars		Sun
06 00 to 07 30	04 30 to 06 00		03 00 to 04 30
Mercury — 07 30 to 09 00			01 30 to 03 00 — Snake
09 00 to 10 30		10 30 to 12 00	12 00 to 01 30
Venus		Saturn	Snake

6. Monday. The 6ᵗʰ Jamam. Time 01 30 to 03 00. Both day and night.

Mars	Sun		Snake
06 00 to 07 30	04 30 to 06 00		03 00 to 04 30
			01 30 to 03 00 / Moon
Jupiter / 07 30 to 09 00			
09 00 to 10 30		10 30 to 12 00	12 00 to 01 30
Mercury		Venus	Saturn

7. **Monday. The 7th Jamam. Time 03 00 to 04 30. Both day and night.**

Sun	Snake		Moon
06 00 to 07 30	04 30 to 06 00		03 00 to 04 30
			01 30 to 03 00 — Saturn
Mars — 07 30 to 09 00			
09 00 to 10 30		10 30 to 12 00	12 00 to 01 30
Jupiter		Mercury	Venus

8. **Monday. The 8ᵗʰ Jamam. Time. 04 30 to 06 00. Both day and night.**

Snake		Moon				Saturn
	06 00 to 07 30	04 30 to 06 00			03 00 to 04 30	
					01 30 to 03 00	Venus
Sun	07 30 to 09 00					
	09 00 to 10 30		10 30 to 12 00		12 00 to 01 30	
Mars				Jupiter		Mercury

1. **Tuesday. The first Jamam. Time 06 00 to 07 30. Both day and night.**

Mars		Sun				Snake
	06 00 to 07 30	04 30 to 06 00			03 00 to 04 30	
					01 30 to 03 00	Moon
Jupiter	07 30 to 09 00					
	09 00 to 10 30			10 30 to 12 00	12 00 to 01 30	
Mercury				Venus		Saturn

2. Tuesday. The second Jamam. Time. 07 30 to 09 00. Both day and night.

Sun		Snake			Moon
	06 00 to 07 30	04 30 to 06 00		03 00 to 04 30	
				01 30 to 03 00	Saturn
Mars	07 30 to 09 00				
	09 00 to 10 30		10 30 to 12 00	12 00 to 01 30	
Jupiter			Mercury		Venus

3. Tuesday. 3rd Jamam. Time 09 00 to 10 30. Both day and night.

Snake	Moon		Saturn
06 00 to 07 30	04 30 to 06 00		03 00 to 04 30
			01 30 to 03 00 / Venus
Sun / 07 30 to 09 00			
09 00 to 10 30		10 30 to 12 00	12 00 to 01 30
Mars		Jupiter	Mercury

4. Tuesday. 4th Jamam. Time. 10 30 to 12 00. Both day and night.

Moon	Saturn		Venus
06 00 to 07 30	04 30 to 06 00		03 00 to 04 30
			01 30 to 03 00 — Mercury
Snake — 07 30 to 09 00			
09 00 to 10 30		10 30 to 12 00	12 00 to 01 30
Sun		Jupiter	Jupiter

5. Tuesday. 5th Jamam. 12 00 to 01 30. Both day and night.

Saturn	Venus		Mercury
06 00 to 07 30	04 30 to 06 00		03 00 to 04 30
			01 30 to 03 00 **Jupiter**
Moon 07 30 to 09 00			
09 00 to 10 30		10 30 to 12 00	12 00 to 01 30
Snake		Sun	Mars

6. Tuesday. 6th Jamam. 01 30 to 03 00. Both day and night.

Venus		Mercury		Jupiter
	06 00 to 07 30	04 30 to 06 00		03 00 to 04 30
				01 30 to 03 00 / Mars
Saturn	07 30 to 09 00			
	09 00 to 10 30		10 30 to 12 00	12 00 to 01 30
Moon			Snake	Sun

7. Tuesday. 7ᵗʰ Jamam. Time 03 00 to 04 30. Both day and night.

Mercury	Jupiter		Mars
06 00 to 07 30	04 30 to 06 00		03 00 to 04 30
		01 30 to 03 00	Sun
Venus 07 30 to 09 00			
09 00 to 10 30	10 30 to 12 00	12 00 to 01 30	
Saturn	Moon		Snake

8. Tuesday. 8th Jamam. Time 04 30 to 06 00. Both day and night.

Jupiter		Mars				Sun
	06 00 to 07 30	04 30 to 06 00			03 00 to 04 30	
					01 30 to 03 00	Snake
Mercury	07 30 to 09 00					
	09 00 to 10 30			10 30 to 12 00	12 00 to 01 30	
Venus				Saturn		Moon

1. Wednesday. 1st Jamam. Time 06 00 to 07 30. Both day and night.

Mercury	Jupiter		Mars
06 00 to 07 30	04 30 to 06 00		03 00 to 04 30
			01 30 to 03 00 — Sun
Venus — 07 30 to 09 00			
09 00 to 10 30		10 30 to 12 00	12 00 to 01 30
Saturn		Moon	Snake

2. Wednesday. 2nd Jamam. Time 07 30 to 09 00. Both day and night.

Jupiter		Mars			Sun
	06 00 to 07 30	04 30 to 06 00		03 00 to 04 30	
				01 30 to 03 00	Snake
Mercury	07 30 to 09 00				
	09 00 to 10 30		10 30 to 12 00	12 00 to 01 30	
Venus			Saturn		Moon

3. Wednesday. 3rd Jamam. Time 09 00 to 10 30. Both day and night.

Mars	Sun		Snake
06 00 to 07 30	04 30 to 06 00		03 00 to 04 30
			01 30 to 03 00 — Moon
Jupiter — 07 30 to 09 00			
09 00 to 10 30		10 30 to 12 00	12 00 to 01 30
Mercury		Venus	Saturn

4. Wednesday. 4th Jamam. Time 10 30 to 12 00. Both day and night.

Sun	Snake		Moon
06 00 to 07 30	04 30 to 06 00		03 00 to 04 30
			01 30 to 03 00
			Saturn
Mars	07 30 to 09 00		
	09 00 to 10 30	10 30 to 12 00	12 00 to 01 30
Jupiter		Mercury	Venus

5. Wednesday. 5th Jamam. Time 12 00 to 01 30. Both day and night.

Snake	Moon		Saturn
06 00 to 07 30	04 30 to 06 00		03 00 to 04 30
Sun 07 30 to 09 00			01 30 to 03 00 Venus
09 00 to 10 30		10 30 to 12 00	12 00 to 01 30
Mars		Jupiter	Mercury

6. Wednesday. 6th Jamam. Time 01 30 to 03 00. Both day and night.

Moon		Saturn			Venus
	06 00 to 07 30	04 30 to 06 00		03 00 to 04 30	
				01 30 to 03 00	Mercury
Snake	07 30 to 09 00				
	09 00 to 10 30		10 30 to 12 00	12 00 to 01 30	
Sun			Mars		Jupiter

7. **Wednesday. 7ᵗʰ Jamam. Time 03 00 to 04 30. Both day and night.**

Saturn		Venus				Mercury
	06 00 to 07 30	04 30 to 06 00		03 00 to 04 30		
				01 30 to 03 00	Jupiter	
Moon	07 30 to 09 00					
	09 00 to 10 30		10 30 to 12 00	12 00 to 01 30		
Snake			Sun		Mars	

8. Wednesday. 8th Jamam. Time 04 30 to 06 00. Both day and night.

Venus		Mercury				Jupiter
	06 00 to 07 30	04 30 to 06 00			03 00 to 04 30	
					01 30 to 03 00	Mars
Saturn	07 30 to 09 00					
	09 00 to 10 30			10 30 to 12 00	12 00 to 01 30	
Moon				Snake		Sun

1. Thursday. 1ˢᵗ Jamam. Time 06 00 to 07 30. Both day and night.

Jupiter	Mars		Sun
06 00 to 07 30	04 30 to 06 00		03 00 to 04 30
			01 30 to 03 00 / Snake
Mercury / 07 30 to 09 00			
09 00 to 10 30		10 30 to 12 00	12 00 to 01 30
Venus		Saturn	Moon

2. Thursday. 2nd Jamam. Time 07 30 to 09 00. Both day and night.

Mars		Sun				Snake
	06 00 to 07 30	04 30 to 06 00			03 00 to 04 30	
					01 30 to 03 00	Moon
Jupiter	07 30 to 09 00					
	09 00 to 10 30			10 30 to 12 00	12 00 to 01 30	
Mercury				Venus		Saturn

3. Thursday. 3rd Jamam. Time 09 00 to 10 30. Both day and night.

Sun	Snake			Moon
06 00 to 07 30	04 30 to 06 00		03 00 to 04 30	
			01 30 to 03 00	Saturn
Mars / 07 30 to 09 00				
09 00 to 10 30		10 30 to 12 00	12 00 to 01 30	
Jupiter		Mercury		Venus

4. Thursday. 4th Jamam. Time 10 30 to 12 00. Both day and night.

Snake		Moon				Saturn
	06 00 to 07 30	04 30 to 06 00			03 00 to 04 30	
					01 30 to 03 00	Venus
Sun	07 30 to 09 00					
	09 00 to 10 30			10 30 to 12 00	12 00 to 01 30	
Mars				Jupiter		Mercury

5. Thursday. 5th Jamam. Time 12 00 to 01 30. Both day and night.

Moon	Saturn		Venus
06 00 to 07 30	04 30 to 06 00	03 00 to 04 30	
		01 30 to 03 00	Mercury
Snake — 07 30 to 09 00			
09 00 to 10 30	10 30 to 12 00	12 00 to 01 30	
Sun	Mars	Jupiter	

6. Thursday. 6th Jamam. Time 01 30 to 03 00. Both day and night.

Saturn		Venus				Mercury
	06 00 to 07 30	04 30 to 06 00			03 00 to 04 30	
					01 30 to 03 00	Jupiter
Moon	07 30 to 09 00					
	09 00 to 10 30		10 30 to 12 00	12 00 to 01 30		
Snake				Sun		Mars

7. **Thursday. 7ᵗʰ Jamam. Time 03 00 to 04 30. Both day and night.**

Venus	Mercury		Jupiter
06 00 to 07 30	04 30 to 06 00	03 00 to 04 30	
		01 30 to 03 00	Mars
Saturn 07 30 to 09 00			
09 00 to 10 30	10 30 to 12 00	12 00 to 01 30	
Moon	Snake		Sun

8. Thursday. 8th Jamam. Time 04 30 to 06 00. Both day and night.

Mercury		Jupiter				Mars
	06 00 to 07 30	04 30 to 06 00			03 00 to 04 30	
					01 30 to 03 00	Sun
Venus	07 30 to 09 00					
	09 00 to 10 30			10 30 to 12 00	12 00 to 01 30	
Saturn				Moon		Snake

1. **Friday. 1ˢᵗ Jamam. Time 06 00 to 07 30. Both day and night.**

Venus		Mercury				Jupiter
	06 00 to 07 30	04 30 to 06 00			03 00 to 04 30	
					01 30 to 03 00	Mars
Saturn	07 30 to 09 00					
	09 00 to 10 30			10 30 to 12 00	12 00 to 01 30	
Moon				Snake		Sun

2. Friday. 2ⁿᵈ Jamam. Time 07 30 to 09 00. Both day and night.

Mercury		Jupiter	Mars
	06 00 to 07 30	04 30 to 06 00		03 00 to 04 30
			01 30 to 03 00	Sun
Venus	07 30 to 09 00			
	09 00 to 10 30		10 30 to 12 00	12 00 to 01 30
Saturn		Moon	Snake

3.   Friday. 3rd Jamam. Time 09 00 to 10 30. Both day and night.

Jupiter	Mars		Sun
06 00 to 07 30	04 30 to 06 00		03 00 to 04 30
			01 30 to 03 00 — Snake
Mercury — 07 30 to 09 00			
09 00 to 10 30		10 30 to 12 00	12 00 to 01 30
Venus	Saturn	Moon	

4. Friday. 4th Jamam. Time 10 30 to 12 00. Both day and night.

Mars	Sun		Snake
06 00 to 07 30	04 30 to 06 00		03 00 to 04 30
			01 30 to 03 00 · Moon
Jupiter · 07 30 to 09 00			
09 00 to 10 30		10 30 to 12 00	12 00 to 01 30
Mercury		Venus	Saturn

5. Friday. 5ᵗʰ Jamam. Time 12 00 to 01 30. Both day and night.

Sun		Snake			Moon
	06 00 to 07 30	04 30 to 06 00		03 00 to 04 30	
				01 30 to 03 00	Saturn
Mars	07 30 to 09 00				
	09 00 to 10 30		10 30 to 12 00	12 00 to 01 30	
Jupiter			Mercury		Venus

6. Friday. 6th Jamam. Time 01 30 to 03 00. Both and night.

Snake		Moon			Saturn
	06 00 to 07 30	04 30 to 06 00		03 00 to 04 30	
				01 30 to 03 00	Venus
Sun	07 30 to 09 00				
	09 00 to 10 30		10 30 to 12 00	12 00 to 01 30	
Mars			Jupiter		Mercury

7. Friday. 7th Jamam. Time 03 00 to 04 30. Both day and night.

Moon		Saturn			Venus
	06 00 to 07 30	04 30 to 06 00		03 00 to 04 30	
				01 30 to 03 00	Mercury
Snake	07 30 to 09 00				
	09 00 to 10 30		10 30 to 12 00	12 00 to 01 30	
Sun			Mars		Jupiter

8. Friday. 8th Jamam. Time 04 30 to 06 00. Both day and night.

Saturn	Venus		Mercury
	06 00 to 07 30	04 30 to 06 00		03 00 to 04 30
			01 30 to 03 00	Jupiter
Moon	07 30 to 09 00		
	09 00 to 10 30		10 30 to 12 00	12 00 to 01 30
Snake		Sun	Mars

1. **Saturday. 1ˢᵗ Jamam. Time 06 00 to 07 30. Both day and night.**

Saturn		Venus			Mercury
	06 00 to 07 30	04 30 to 06 00		03 00 to 04 30	
				01 30 to 03 00	Jupiter
Moon	07 30 to 09 00				
	09 00 to 10 30		10 30 to 12 00	12 00 to 01 30	
Snake			Sun		Mars

2. Saturday. 2nd Jamam. Time 07 30 to 09 00. Both day and night.

Venus	Mercury		Jupiter
06 00 to 07 30	04 30 to 06 00		03 00 to 04 30
			01 30 to 03 00 / Mars
Saturn / 07 30 to 09 00			
09 00 to 10 30		10 30 to 12 00	12 00 to 01 30
Moon		Snake	Sun

3. Saturday. 3rd Jamam. Time. 09 00 to 10 30. Both day and night.

Mercury	Jupiter		Mars
06 00 to 07 30	04 30 to 06 00		03 00 to 04 30
			01 30 to 03 00 · Sun
Venus · 07 30 to 09 00			
09 00 to 10 30		10 30 to 12 00	12 00 to 01 30
Saturn		Moon	Snake

4. Saturday. 4th Jamam. Time 10 30 to 12 00. Both day and night.

Jupiter		Mars				Sun
	06 00 to 07 30	04 30 to 06 00			03 00 to 04 30	
					01 30 to 03 00	Snake
Mercury	07 30 to 09 00					
	09 00 to 10 30		10 30 to 12 00	12 00 to 01 30		
Venus			Saturn			Moon

5. Saturday. 5th Jamam. Time 12 00 to 01 30. Both day and night.

Mars		Sun			Snake
	06 00 to 07 30	04 30 to 06 00		03 00 to 04 30	
				01 30 to 03 00	Moon
Jupiter	07 30 to 09 00				
	09 00 to 10 30		10 30 to 12 00	12 00 to 01 30	
Mercury			Venus		Saturn

6. **Saturday. 6ᵗʰ Jamam. Time 01 30 to 03 00. Both day and night.**

Sun		Snake				Moon
	06 00 to 07 30	04 30 to 06 00			03 00 to 04 30	
					01 30 to 03 00	Saturn
Mars	07 30 to 09 00					
	09 00 to 10 30			10 30 to 12 00	12 00 to 01 30	
Jupiter				Mercury		Venus

7.   **Saturday. 7ᵗʰ Jamam. Time 03 00 to 04 30. Both day and night.**

Snake		Moon			Saturn
	06 00 to 07 30	04 30 to 06 00		03 00 to 04 30	
				01 30 to 03 00	Venus
Sun	07 30 to 09 00				
	09 00 to 10 30		10 30 to 12 00	12 00 to 01 30	
Mars			Jupiter		Mercury

8. **Saturday. 8ᵗʰ Jamam. Time 04 30 to 06 00. Both day and night.**

Moon		Saturn				Venus
	06 00 to 07 30	04 30 to 06 00		03 00 to 04 30		
				01 30 to 03 00	Mercury	
Snake	07 30 to 09 00					
	09 00 to 10 30		10 30 to 12 00	12 00 to 01 30		
Sun			Mars		Jupiter	

These are the Jamakkol chart arrangements for the seven days of the week and for the corresponding eight Jamam timings.

7. Timing of the Prasanam

In prasanam the time is the notable and crucial factor to arrive at the results. In the Horary or the Prasanna astrology, the time of the question of the querist is very important. This time is reckoned as equivalent to the birth time of a baby in the natal horoscope. When the client comes and meets the astrologer in person, the time of his query and the instant of answering it will be almost the same. So there is no dispute here. But when the questions are asked by letter or by using phones or mobile devices or other social media channels, the astrologer may not see them immediately. He would open the letter after he receives it. In the social media messages also he would go through them only when he is free. And there is a time delay happening in all these situations between the time the question is raised and the time the astrologer analyses or answers it. This time delay may vary from a few hours to even a few days. And now which time the astrologer should consider? The time of the question or the time now he sits for analysing it.

The astrologer should take the time of his analysis as the time of the Prasanam. He should never consider the time of the query. So it is always advised in the Jamakkol Prasanam that the actual time of the analysis is the exact time of the prasanam. This is the golden rule about the Timing used.

Similarly, the place of the Prasanam is to be taken as the place where the astrologer is based and doing his calculations. For distant calls or even queries from abroad clients, the astrologer need not take their place as the base. It is always the place from where he is analysing now. The planetary position of that place is to be used.

8. Transit Planets

Using a standard panchang, the position of all the transit planets for that date of the Prasanna can be found out. And then they are recorded in the chart. The transit planets are written inside the zodiac squares, as usual. The details like the Retrograde state, the Combustion, the

Exchange of the planetary houses and also the status of the planets whether they are exalted or in debilitated houses have also to be noted. The degree wise placement of the planets inside the rasis will help for accurate predictions. The first duty of the astrologer on every day morning, as every one of us know and agree and also doing daily is to consult a Panchang and note the planetary positions of that day. This simple and routine preparation is the handy aid and the helping arsenal for the astrological calculations and the predictions.

A planet may be exalted in the birth chart but it may be found debilitated in the transit or vice versa. Similarly, the status of the position of the planets may be the same or different in the transit. All these have to have carefully scrutinized as each and every one of these has a bearing on the prediction of the results.

9. Kaarakathuvas

The Kaarakathuvas is one area which we are concentrating and updating in every one of our books. If these are properly understood, the prediction becomes precise and perfect.

The Kaarakathuvas or the Significators are defined as the nature, attribute, representation, quality and/or the property of the planets, rasis and the bhavas. There are separate kaarakathuvas for the stars also. These are listed in many of the astrological books both old and the new. The Uthra kalamirtham by Shri Kalidasa gives a detailed study of the Kaarakathuvas. The astrologers are expected to have a thorough understanding of the Kaarakathuvas. This alone is not sufficient. The astrologer must know how to use them properly. We will discuss how these kaarakathuvas can be interpreted and applied in the day to day predictions. While introducing the wonderful technique of Jamakkol prasanam, we have tried to throw some light on the subject of Kaarakathuvas. Instead of merely listing of the entities, special emphasis has been given to appreciate, interpret and use the Kaarakathuvas most effectively.

In Uthra Kalamirtham, Shri Kalidasa notes that ghee is one of the kaarakathuvas of the Seventh house. Simply reading it and knowing this alone is not going to help. We must know how to use this. Suppose the 7th house or its lord is connected with the Lagna or the Lagna lord, then we can say that the native is fond of food dishes made out of ghee. Similarly, if the 7th bhava is connected to the 10th house or its lord, then we can conclude that the native can do the business related to the ghee.

In another example, in the same classical work, Shri Kalidasa says, thorny tree is one of the Kaarakathuvas for the Sun. How to understand this. Nobody dares to go near a thorny tree as it will prick and harm them. Similarly, going nearer to a King, (represented by the Sun) is always risky. The proximity could damage them one day or the other. In today's context, we can substitute the politicians or the Government officials, instead of the King.

In the Bhava Kaarakathuvas, the third house is allocated to the younger coborn. Now, what does this signify. On the face of it nothing. But it illustrates that the age difference for the next coborn should be three years. Similarly, why the fifth bhava denotes the children. Because it is the 11th house, the house of Gains for the 7th house, the house of marriage.

Similarly, many things are embedded in the Kaarakathuvas. Each and every one of them can be analysed. If only the Kaarakathuvas are mastered, the science of astrology itself can be clearly understood. They are the fundamental blocks. Herewith in this book, the detailed list of the Kaarakathuvas of the planets, the rasis and the bhavas is given. This organized list of the kaarakathuvas is the updated one and it is relevant to the needs of today. Also it will serve as an eye opener and guidance for further research on the subject of the Kaarakathuvas. They need through inspection, introspection and insight to decipher the messages engrained in the kaarakathuvas and also in the rules and the principles of astrology. On the face of it, they may not give the direct meaning. Only a thorough knowledge and inquisitiveness will open up the hidden treasures.

For example, in a section of the society, the physical contact between the newly married couples is forbidden in the Tamil month of Aadi. This month will correspond roughly to the 15th of July to the 15th of August. It has not been explained why. Some of the interpretations run like this. If they join in that period, the child might have born in April. And April is the peak of the summer and the new born and the mother will suffer in that hot weather.

But, the astrological view in this episode is more clear and meaningful. Suppose, they join in July, and the fetus is formed, it will be the fourth month of growth for it in the month of October. The October month represents the Thula rasi where the Sun gets debilitated. In the correlation between the development of the fetus and the planets, the Sun is the planet in charge of the fourth month. The Sun is the kaaraka for the major and the vital organs like the heart, the spinal cord, the bones, the eyes etc., So these organs might not get fully developed or might suffer from malfunctions when the Sun is in its weaker state. That's why the July ban has been in vogue. Furthermore, the planet responsible for the fifth month is the Moon, which gets debilitated in the next house, the Virschika rasi.

Thus many of the things found in the astrological parlance like the rules, bhavas, planets, the formation and the arrangement of the houses and the rasis, etc. have deeper meaning and definable logic.

The Rasi, the Bhava and the Nakshtra kaarakathuvas are dealt separately in a subsequent chapter.

10. The Rays or the Rasmi

The intensity of the planets is symbolically represented in terms of numbers which are called as the Rasmi or the Rays. The rasmi is used wherever there is a numerical calculation or numerical involvement.

For example, queries involving the cost of any particle or property, the distance, the size, the time of fructification of results, age, number of persons, etc., the rasmi gives an idea of the numerical value. There are Rasmi values attributed to all the nine planets and also to the twelve rasis.

Number	Planet	Rasmi or rays	In own house (double)	In exalted house (triple)
1	Sun	05	10	15
2	Moon	21	42	63
3	Mars	08	24	24
4	Mercury	16	32	48
5	Jupiter	10	20	30
6	Venus	20	40	60
7	Saturn	04	08	12
8	Rahu	04	-	-
9	Ketu	04	-	-

In the houses of their debilitation, the value of the rasmi becomes zero for all the planets.

Number	Rasi	Rasmi or rays	Age indicated by the Rasi
01	Mesha	08	28.5
02	Rishaba	08	17.5
03	Mithuna	05	33.5
04	Kataka	03	40.5
05	Simha	08	28.5
06	Kanya	11	17.5
07	Thula	02	33.5
08	Virschika	04	40.5
09	Dhanus	06	28.5
10	Makara	08	17.5
11	Kumbha	08	33.5
12	Meena	27	40.5

How the age is calculated using the Rasmi? In the Mesha the stars Ashwini 4 padha, Bharani 4 padha and Kirthikai first padha are present. The Vimsottari dasa years of the Ketu is 7, the Sukra is 20 years and the Sun is 6 years. Since only one padha of the Sun's star is present in the Mesha rasi, we take only the 25 percent of the dasa period of the Sun at the Mesha. So the age mentioned in the Mesha is 7 plus 20 plus 1.5 = 28.5 years. Similarly, for the Rishaba, applying the same calculations, it is 4.5 plus 10 plus 3 = 17.5 years. And this goes on for all the other signs in the same way.

The Rules of the Jamakkol Prasanam

1. The Jama planet in the Udhaya indicates the mind of the querist. The kaarakathuvam of that planet will be his question.

2. The Jama planet in the 10th house or the 10th bhava confirms the first rule.

3. The planet or the Bhava in the Kavippu indicates the hidden things, secrets, losses associated with the question.

Rule 1

The Jama planets means the planets placed outside the zodiac square. With Mesha as the example for Udhaya lagna, the Rule 1 is discussed with reference to the Kaarakathuvas of the various Jama planets placed outside the Mesha Udhaya. This is true for all the 12 udhaya lagnas. We will take the planets one by one placed in the Mesha udhaya.

1. The Sun in the Udhaya lagna

Suppose the Sun is the planet located in the outer circle of the Udhaya lagna. Now the questions from the client will be regarding his father, father in law, the Government, the eyes, the heart, permanent income, the eldest son, the gold, the heredity, the prestige, the honour, the honesty, the administration, the hilly terrain, etc.,

In this example, the Sun is the 5th bhava lord for the Mesha Udhaya. Then the Kaarakathuvas of that Fifth bhava will also find a part in the question. The native may ask about his ancestry, about his family deity, about his maternal uncle, about his children, about his stomach ailments, about his recreational activities, about share markets, etc., all the important kaaraka of the fifth bhava.

In this example of the Mesha udhaya the Sun is exalted here. So the kaaraka of the Sun will attain success here in this Jama arrangement. Of course, the position of the Kavippu also has to be considered.

2. The Moon in the Udhaya

Now Moon is the Jama planet placed outside the Udhaya. Now the questions from the client will be related to the Moon and/or the 4th bhava.

The mother, the mother in law, the mind, the food, the depreciation, the movements and changes like the travel or the transfer, blood circulation, some theft activities, white substances like the milk, cotton, liquid items, liquor, products and professions connected with the sea, conceptions, child birth, movable and immovable properties, pet animals, cattle rearing, the heart, the lungs, watery areas, etc. will be the subject of the queries here.

	Moon		
	Udhaya		

3. The Mars in the Udhaya

In this case, the Mars is the Jama planet placed outside the Udhaya. So the kaaraka of the Mars will be the predominant questions. The house, the land, the brothers, the diseases, uniformed services, the surgery, the accidents, the fire, the weapons, the agricultural lands, buildings, adamant nature, ego, adventures, sports, quarrels, disputes, competitions, bones, teeth, etc., form the basis of the query.

	Mars			
	Udhaya			

4. The Mercury in the Udhaya

Here the Mercury is the Jama planet situated outside the Udhaya. The education, academic institutions, accounts, auditing, brokerage, instalments, maternal uncles, friends, lovers, love, younger sister, the skin, the nervous system, the banks, the communication aids and the communication channels, courier service, postal department, records, documents, libraries, books, ambassadors, plans, agencies, etc. will be the part of the native's query.

	Mercury			
	Udhaya			

5. The Jupiter in the Udhaya

Now the Jupiter is the Jama planet positioned outside the Udhaya. The Jupiter is considered to be the most auspicious and benevolent planet. Therefore, the presence of the Jupiter in the Udhaya indicates propitious and positive results. The notable kaarakathuvas of the Guru like the child, the monetary matters, the wealth, the honesty, the virtuous deeds, the divinity, the dignity, the discipline, the learned, the gold, the turmeric, the religious institutions, the judicial academies, the financial organisations, the educational establishments, the brain, the liver, etc., might be the subject of the queries.

	Jupiter			
	Udhaya			

6. The Venus in the Udhaya

Here the Venus is the Jama planet which is posted outside the Udhaya. The Venus always indicates the comforts, the luxury, the elegance, the beauty, the attractiveness, the womenfolk particularly the wife, the elder sister, the aunts, the hormone secretions, the silver articles, the silky, the stylish and the shining costumes, the ornaments, the beautifications, the sophisticated vehicles, poetry, music, arts, drama, cinema, recreational activities, conjugal life, etc., and these kaaraka form the part of the queries.

7. The Saturn in the udhaya.

Now we have the Saturn placed as the Jama planet outside the Udhaya. The Saturn is the planet for the Profession. So whenever the Saturn appears in the Udhaya, the foremost queries will be regarding the profession only. "Can I start a new business or an additional one or switch over to other alternate business. My business is not doing well etc. When will I get a job" are some of the frequent questions when the Saturn is in the Udhaya.

Now when we have the Saturn placed as the Jama planet outside the Udhaya, the questions related to the other main kaaraka for the Saturn, the longevity also arise. So the queries will be based on these. The questions on the health and the longevity of the sick might be asked. Depending upon the status of the Saturn and the position of the Kavippu, these queries can be answered. Queries regarding health, nature of illness, chances of recovery, time of recovery, whether recovery will be there or not etc., can be handled.

The Saturn is a slow moving planet. So when the Saturn appears in the Udhayam it indicates a certain amount of delay in the fructification of the results. The legs, the dull aching pains, the servants, the handicapped persons, the younger brother of the father, the coal, the dirty and the ugly things, the hard labour, the slavery, the night time, the dejections, the disappointments, the elderly look, the renunciation, the broken and the waste, etc., are the part of the queries.

	Saturn		
	Udhaya		

8. The Snake in the Udhaya

In this case, the Snake is the Jama planet which is located outside the Udhaya. The presence of the Snake in the Udhaya generally indicates crisis, calamity, critical situations, dangers and such inauspicious things only. But, there are some particular circumstances during which the Snake indicates positive and favourable results.

1. When the native asks anything about going to distant places or foreign lands.

2. When the question is about bore well installation

3. And when someone asks about child birth the presence of the snake in the Udhaya or in the 2nd house, 5th house or the 9th house indicates the definite possibility of begetting a child. Depending upon the position of the Kavippu, it might indicate whether the child birth is through natural means or by artificial methods.

	Snake		
	Udhaya		

Rule 2

The planet in the 10th house will spell-out the mind of the native.

The planet in the 10th house is used to identify the query when the client has not volunteered to open his mind/mouth. And in case, when the question has been asked straight, the planet in the 10th bhava is used to confirm it. Moreover, it is also useful to find out whether the query will get fructify or not. We have just studied in Rule number 1, that the Kaaraka of the planet in the Udhaya lagna will be helpful to identify the question. Rule 2 says that similar thing can be found from the 10th house. Now which is true. The fact is that both are true. The planet in the Udhaya will act according to its kaaraka and/or the bhava placement. It will command or control the native to do a particular act. Whereas the planet in the 10th house will substantiate the planet in the Udhaya. And more than that, it will simply suggest to do a certain thing, but will not press hard on it.

Rule 3

The placement of the Kavippu with reference to the Udhaya lagna will indicate the secrets involved in the Prasanam.

The bhava in which the Kavippu is placed will indicate the bitterness, difficulties, losses, anguishes, delays, diseases, the disappointments and the hidden things related to the query and its chances of fulfillment or not.

When the Kavippu is placed in a certain Bhava, it can be inferred that the native is suffering due to the kaaraka of that bhava. The body part indicted by that bhava could be the diseased organ in the queries regarding the health. The native will not have cordial relations or get separated from those relatives indicated by the bhava kaarakathuvam afflicted by the Kavippu.

More importantly, if the Kavippu falls on the bhava or if the Kavippu affects the kaaraka planet which is related to the present query of the client, then, it can be ascertained that the native will face suffering, loss or failure connected to this particular pursuit. The Kavippu, as we have seen, indicates the darker and the hidden things of the life. The Kavippu is like a murky cloud. It engulfs the planet or the bhava with which it gets into contact. With this understanding, we will proceed to discuss the role of Kavippu and the placement of it in the various houses from the Udhaya elaborately.

1. The Kavippu is placed in the Udhaya.

So the query will be about the client himself. The bhava and the kaaraka of the first house gets affected. This will also indicate the diseases in the body parts denoted by the first bhava. For example, since the Mesha udhaya refers to the head, the native might be suffering from the diseases like the head ache, brain disorders, migraine, hair fall, etc., Since the Kavippu is in the Udhaya itself, it indicates that the native is suffering at that present period of time. It will be hell of a life situation for him. His condition will be worse and he would feel like to be in the claws and the clutches of a devil. And, unfortunately, his questions about himself will not meet with success.

Udhaya
Kavippu

2. The Kavippu in the 2nd house.

The questions from the client will be related to the kaaraka of the 2nd bhava, like the family, the face, the speech, the eyes, the finances (Dhana sthana), addition of new members in the family (may be the spouse or the child), basic education etc., But these kaarakathuvas would have been affected or going to get disturbed when the Kavippu is in the 2nd bhava. For example, if the native asks about getting money or expecting his/her life partner or a child as a new inclusion in his/her life, the answers turn to be negative. It's either delayed or denied.

	Udhaya	Kavippu

3. The Kavippu in the 3rd house.

Some of the notable kaaraka of the third bhava are the younger coborn, the communication, the displacements, the valour, the vigour, the ears, the short journeys etc. The native will face problems of failures in these areas and also in the other significators of the 3rd house.

	Udhaya		Kavippu	

4. The Kavippu in the 4th house.

The 4th house denotes the mother as the chief kaaraka. Among the other karakas, the vehicles, the landed property, the house, the heart, the pet animals, the domestic animals, the water sources, the education, the cheerfulness are the notable ones. When the Kavippu is in the 4th house these significators suffer. For example, the native's mother becomes ill. The native met with a vehicle accident. His cattle get lost or die. The native suffers from heart related ailments. His plan to buy the lands or construct a house gets delayed or disturbed. The fourth house in a way refers to the security as the mother protects her children. So when the 4th house is afflicted by the presence of the Kavippu, the native feels helplessness and hopelessness.

	Udhaya			
			Kavippu	

5. The Kavippu in the 5th house.

The 5th house is the kaaraka for the progeny, the ancestry, the share market, imagination, love, recreations, the Kula deiva, initiation and the invocation of Mantras, the writing of books, the stomach, the maternal uncle, etc. These are the few of the prominent Kaaraka of the 5th bhava. Generally, the 5th house is a Trikona. And when the Trikona house is getting affected by the placement of the Kavippu there at this significant house. The progeny is either delayed or denied. The love is met with failure. The stomach ailments trouble the native and so on and so forth like this. The creativity and the inspiration gets evaporated.

Udhaya

Kavippu

6. The Kavippu in the 6th house.

The 6th house is noted for the three important karakas the Runa (the debts), the Roga (the diseases) and the Chatru (the enmity). Naturally the placement of the Kavippu in the 6th house will make the native suffer due to these three elements, one or all. If the planet Guru or the Mercury is associated with the 6th house, then it is financial debts. If it is the Saturn, then it is the diseases. The Mars will invite the hostility. The court litigations will also torment the native. The Ketu will have his hand here. Some people may be robbed off and some may even get imprisoned. The lower abdomen and the liver may get affected. The servants and the routine job are denoted by the 6th bhava. So the servants will betray or the good servants will leave the native. The attitude and the attachment of the native towards his duty and work will turn adverse.

7. The Kavippu in the 7th house.

The marital life and the life partner, the social recognition of the man to woman relationship by way of the marriage, business partners, the customers or the clients in the business, proper or legalized conjugal life, the kidneys, the negotiations, the remedies, etc., are the noteworthy karakas for the 7th bhava. When the Kavippu is placed in the 7th house and the question is asked whether this marriage will take place or not, then the answer is a clear No. If it is the same situation in a married man or woman's chart, the partner will get separated or will pass away.

Udhaya

Kavippu

8. The Kavippu in the 8th house.

The 8th house is dreaded by some people as it is connected with the longevity and also the slandering of one's name and fame. Unexpected monetary gains are indicated by this house only. For example, gains through the lottery, races, the treasure, compensation from the Insurance, inheritance through the will and gambling are denoted. The privy parts are represented by this house. And the presence of the Kavippu here brings illness in those areas. Separation in married life occurs for a few. The native behaves lazy and troubled by the mounting debts. He lives like a slave or like a refugee who has lost everything. Unexpected death is also indicted. Starts to the addiction of drinks or drugs.

9. The Kavippu in the 9th house.

The chief kaaraka of this house are the father, paternal property, pilgrimages, long journeys, sea voyages, temple related works like the construction, charitable deeds, interest in holy scriptures, the thighs, the higher education, spiritual inclinations, the second marriage, the third child and legal matters. When the Kavippu is placed in the 9th bhava, these kaarakathuvas are getting affected. Suppose the client asks, "Can I go for this pilgrimage?", then the answer will be a definite No. Will my father give this to me is the question? The answer is he will not.

Udhaya

Kavippu

10. The Kavippu in the 10th house.

This house represents the most important aspect of a human life. How he is earning his livelihood. What is his profession or business? Also it denotes the final rites one is performing for the dead. The 10th house also represents the authority, postings, favour from the Government, government jobs, name and fame, the status, the social recognition, the knees in the human body.

11. The Kavippu in the 11th house.

The 11th house is called the Labha sthana, the house of gains. When this house is getting affected by the presence of the Kavippu there, the damage is more. The elder brothers, the friends, the gains or the happiness of the life, left ear, the ankles are referred by the 11th house. The 11th house indicates the success for any enterprise. When the Kavippu is placed there, the task does not get succeed. The presence of the Kavippu in the 2nd house and the 11th house brings fall and failure in all the pursuits the native wants to proceed.

12. The Kavippu in the 12th house.

The 12th house is the house of expenses, loss, exile, hospitalization, imprisonment, the Moksha, etc., The kaaraka will get affected when the Kavippu is in the 12th house. Suppose the native asks about whether he can go to a foreign country or whether he would get Permanent residence (green card) status and the Kavippu is placed in the 12th house, the answer indicates a negative outcome only. The 12th house indicates the conjugal pleasures. If there is a disharmony between the couple and the Kavippu is in the12th house during the query related to them, then it indicates that everything is not well in their physical relationship.

Kavippu	Udhaya		

We have seen the effects, rather, the ill effects of the presence of the Kavippu makes in the twelve houses. Similarly, the effects of the Kavippu when it is present with the 9 planets are elucidated now.

1. The Sun in the Kavippu.

Now we have the Kavippu and the Sun together. When the native asks anything about his father or the father in law or his eldest son or any query about the Government or the politicians or his right eye or about his permanent income, then the answers are negative. Suppose he asks, whether his father will recover from the illness, then the answer is he will not get cured.

Likewise, the other Kaaraka of the Sun like, the administration, the Saivite worship, the wheat, the Jwellery business, the allopathic doctor, the heart, the spinal cord, etc., will get affected when the Sun is in the Kavippu. If the question is raised about the father neither the Sun nor the 9th house nor the 9th lord should be with the Kavippu. Also to be noted that the presence of the above planets like the Sun or the 9th lord, in the internal or the external sign in the sign where the Kavippu is located yields the same result. The same is true for all the other planets, the kaaraka and the bhava lords respectively.

Sun

Kavippu

2. The Moon in the Kavippu.

The Moon is the chief kaaraka for the mother and the Mind. The Moon denotes food and nourishment, travels, the uterus, the mother in law, the watery resources, milk and its products, all the things we get from the sea like the salt, fish, conch shells etc., and all the professions connected with the sea from the fishing to the sailing, the lungs, the respiratory disorders, the digestive system etc., When the Kavippu affects the Moon these kaarakathuvas are getting afflicted and any query relating them does not succeed.

The mother is affected when the Moon or the 4th bhava or the 4th bhava lord is connected with the Kavippu.

	Moon		
	Kavippu		

3. The Mars in the Kavippu.

The Mars is the Karaka for the brother, the husband, the blood, the fire, the weapons, the machinery, the uniformed professions like the police, the military, the fire service personnel, the electricity board employees, the security persons, the boxers, the sports persons, the landed property etc., When the Mars is affected by the Kavippu, these kaarakathuvas are troubled and any query related to them is affected. Suppose, the native asks whether I can buy or construct a house? Or whether my brother will go to foreign? Or can we undergo this surgery? Whether police will help us? Or can I participate in the sports? All these questions are related to the Mars and eventually all of them will met with failure only.

	Mars		
	Kavippu		

4. The Mercury in the Kavippu.

The Mercury is the Kaaraka for the communication. So any question regarding the communication, communication aids, communication business like the courier, online trading, social media such as the WhatsApp or Facebook or e mail and in addition to the traditional communication services like the postal department will not give successful results. The education, the computing talents, the auditing profession, the agency business, the maternal uncle, the books and magazines, the vacant lands, the younger sister are some more kaarakathuvas of the Mercury which will get affected by the presence of Kavippu along with the Mercury.

	Mercury			
	Kavippu			

5. The Jupiter in the Kavippu.

The Jupiter is the most benevolent of the planets. It bestows the auspiciousness on the human life. It is the Kaaraka for the children, the spirituality, the justice, the gold Jwellery, the share market, the bank, the divinity, the discipline, the diligence, the dutiful, the brain, the liver, the gall bladder, the jaundice, the heritage, the magnanimity, the wealth, the propitious things are some of the other things denoted by the Jupiter. Suppose the questions are asked regarding those kaarakathuvas, the things will get defeated. In addition to this, when the Kavippu is on the Jupiter generally demoralizes or demolishes the general good conduct and the character of the native.

	Jupiter		
	Kavippu		

6. The Venus in the Kavippu.

The Venus is the planet for the luxury and the enjoyment. The Venus is the planet for the attraction and the beauty. The Venus denotes the wife, the elder sister, the aunts, the perfumes, the consumer durable equipment, the sophisticated vehicles, the palatial buildings the shining articles (the Rahu and the Venus denotes the shiny and glittering costumes. The Guru and the Bhudha represent the sober and pleasant dresses),

	Mars		
	Kavippu		

7. The Saturn in the Kavippu.

The Saturn is the planet who justifies the effects of ones Karma. The Jupiter analyses ones good and bad karma and writes his judgement based on them. The next dasa lord is the Saturn. He is the implementer of the verdict of the Jupiter on the person's life. The Saturn controls the important element of one's life - the source for his livelihood. It may be a job or business or profession and it may be small or big and it may give adequate or not so adequate or surpluses. Some may work hard and earn little while few others reap huge benefits for their small contribution. All these things are the handiwork of the Saturn.

When the Saturn is affected by the Kavippu, naturally there is a stagnation and struggle in his occupation. The other Kaaraka the longevity is getting affected, especially when the query happens to be about the health and the diseased condition.

Saturn

Kavippu

8. The Snake in the Kavippu.

In the Jamakkol Prasanna system, the Snake is nothing but the Rahu and the Ketu put together as a single component. So when the Snake gets entangled with the Kavippu, the karakas of the two shadowy planets, the Rahu and the Ketu gets a beating. These two planets indicate the ancestors, the Muslim and the Christianity respectively, the crossing of the boundaries, foreign languages, electronics, black magic activities, skin diseases, glittering objects, pawn broker business, about poisons, lawyers, tailoring shops, winding works, commodities like the tobacco, the coffee seeds, the tea leaves, the cotton, the spirituality etc., These are some of the notable kaarakathuvas of the Snake. When the query from the native concerns these and the other kaarakathuvas of the Snake, the answer indicates a negative outcome.

	Snake		
	Kavippu		

It can be seen from the above charts that how the Kavippu encompasses its negativity and unpleasantness on the planets which are afflicted by it. The karakas of the planets met with an adverse situation and face failure and dejection.

Guidelines of the Jamakkol Prasanam

General principles of the Jamakkol prasanam.

This is with reference to the Udhaya lagna. These are the standard planetary positions and their effects in the Jamakkol prasanam. The position of the Aarudam and the Kavippu have to be correlated with the principles stated here.

The Sukra in the first house	Good for wealth, flirting nature
The Sukra in the 2nd house	Illegal contacts
The Sukra in the 10th house	Second half of the life wealthy
The Chandra in the 4th house	Good residence. Conflict with the mother
The Chevvai in the 6th house	Pugnacious. No cordiality between the couple.
The Sun in 7th or the 10th house	No ancestral property
The Chevvai and the Chandra combination	Interest in agriculture.
The Chevvai and the Chandra combination with the aspect of the Guru	The native will do agricultural activities
The Chevvai, the Chandra and the Ketu combination	No interest in the marital life
The Chevvai, the Chandra and the Sukra combination	Illegal contacts exist
The Chevvai, the Chandra and the Bhudha combination	Cowardly nature
The Sukra and the Sani combination	Wealthy status.
The Chandra, the Sukra, the Sani and the Rahu combination	Disgusting diseases
The Guru in the 7th house	The curse of the saintly people
The 10th lord in the 3rd house	Profession not in the native place
The Chandra, the Guru and the Rahu combination	Food poisoning. Food contamination.

Continued…

A Debilitated planet in the 10th house	Comfort less life. Could not be able to enjoy even own property or things.
The Chandra in the 8th house in the gochara	Confused and indecisive.
The Chandra, the Sani and the Rahu combination	Will go to foreign lands. These three planets indicate travelling.
The Chandra, the Bhudha, the Guru and the Ketu combination	Delay or denial of the marriage
The Guru and the Ketu combination	Marriage gets delayed
The Surya, the Chandra, the Bhudha and the Guru combination	Love marriage
The 2nd lord in the 9th or the 11th house	Two marriages.
The 8th lord in the 8th house	Wherever he goes, he will return to his native.
The dasa of the 6th lord	Loss. Will file Insolvency. Debts or diseases.
The 6th and the 8th lord in the 12th house	Lustful and perverted behaviour
The Sani in the 8th house. In gochara also when the Saturn transits the 8th house	Greedy. Will quarrel even with own mentor.
The Chevvai in the 2nd house	Too much of anger
The Guru in the 3rd house	Will not help even his younger brother. Ear problems exist
The Surya in the 11th house	Fruitful for all pursuits. Good position.
The Chevvai in the 8th house	Indecisive or decides wrong
The Sani in the 3rd house or retrograde planets in the 3rd H	Studies interrupted
The Surya and the Chandra combination	There will be a separated husband or wife in the family
The Guru and the Chandra combination	Good for financial matters. But personal life is bitter. Brother's life is affected. Indicates Puthra dosha
The Bhudha in the 5th or 11th house	Astrological talent
The Snake in the 9th or the 10th house	Black magic expert
The Chandra and the Sukra in exchange	Too many contacts. Not good for financial position.
The Chevvai and the Bhudha combination	Engineering education, drinking habits, love while studying,
The Chandra, the Bhudha and the Sukra combination	Covetous, lecherous

The Chandra debilitated and Chevvai combination	Indulge in vices
The Bhudha and the Guru combination	Expert in education, too many friends
The Sukra in the 3rd house	Illegal contacts, Suspicious mind
Debilitated Saturn	Not good for own business. Should employ only few employees in their concern. Need always partners in business.
The Chandra and the Ketu combination	Anxiety, depression
The retrograde planet in the 10th house Or the 10th lord retrograde	Could not run his business alone
The Chandra in 4, 6, 8 or 12th house	Should not do own business or with own capital
The 8th lord in the 7th house	Severe back pain
The 7th lord in the 5th	Risk for marriage life as it moves towards the 6th
The Retrograde Saturn in the 5th H	Troubles with the servants, No maternal uncle
The Mercury exalted	Possess landed property. Good compatibility between the couple.
The Mars, the Venus and the Moon combination	Illicit relationship. Extra marital affair.
The dasa of the 6th lord or the Mercury (the Mercury is the 6th lord of the Kaala Purusha)	Debts increase. Some will file insolvency or gets absconded
The Chevvai in the10th H	Own business is indicated.
The Mars in the 5th H	The native's life prospers after the demise of the father
6th lord debilitated	Could not enjoy the stolen property or the goods.
The Rahu in the Aarudam	Shows a separated wife
8th lord debilitated	Longevity gets affected
No planets in the 5, 7 or at 9 to the Guru	Longevity disturbed. Diseases haunt.
7th lord debilitated	No partner in life or business
Chevvai, Sani and Rahu combination	Indicates major accidents
Combusted Venus	Troubles to the wife, eyes, hormonal system. Delayed marriage.
1st and 7th lords in 6 or 8 or 12th H	Troubled marital life

Continued...

Moon and the Mercury combined	Depression or tension exists
Guru in the 8th	Very adamant
4th and the 8th lords combined	Accidents due to cattle or vehicles
The Mars in the 3rd H	Over confident. Daring.
The lagna and the Saturn within 3 degrees	Short span of life
Mandhi and the Saturn within 3 degrees	Short span of life
Saturn and the Guru	Will go to job at a very early age. Will be the bread winner of the family. Nervous disturbances occur
The Moon debilitated in the 10th H	Will not be able to repay the loans
The 7th lord debilitated in the 10th H	Loan repayment is difficult
Saturn in the 4th H or 4th lord debilitated or debilitated planet in the 4th	They will trust someone and gets betrayed by them

The Nature and the Colour of the Dress

The Jamakkol Prasanam uses the colour and the quality of the dress of the querist as an additional tool in making the predictions. Many things can be inferred from these two. This is true for all types of Prasanam. And in Jamakkol prasanam also, it is being used to gather more information. The fundamental features of the Jamakkol prasanam are more than enough for all types of predictions. But these simple things give supplementary, relevant and valuable details. For example, we can identify the colour of the attire the missing person was wearing last. The probable colour of the costume of the person who is expected to arrive can be inferred. By using Jamakkol prasanam whether a person will come or not can be decided. The experience and the expertise of the astrologer can also determine what would be the colour of his dress. The colour of the dress of the Deity in those prasanam involving them. The favourable colour of the dress for a person who is going to attend an interview or an examination or for a patient who is going to undergo treatment. If someone calls you over the phone, you can tell what was the colour of the dress he was wearing at that time. In prasanam many things like this can be accurately predicted. Like what food the person has taken, in which direction he was sitting when calling through phone etc., Of course, these little things not only speak of the acumen of the astrologer, but also provide further information to the main query. These will enhance the accuracy of the query. The colour of the dresses and their nature attributed to the nine planets are as follows.

The Sun

Light shades of orange and the red, well pressed and creased dresses, white, the dresses one is expected to wear as per his profession (the doctors in white), Jeans and such rough materials and woolen clothes. The Mars also refers to uniformed dresses. But that uniform indicates the dresses of the working people, while the Sun refers to the elite category of the people.

The Moon

Grey, navy blue, cotton white, cotton and khadhi materials, light shades of black, towels, swimming suits, night gowns and all such dresses that are used as night ware.

The Mars

The dark red, brown, very dark shades, the uniform dresses of all the jobs like driver, policemen, military, fire service, postal department, catering services, petrol bunk staff etc.,

The Mercury

Light green, olive green, peach, biscuit and such eye catching and pleasant colours, wet dresses, dresses that are not completely dried, dresses related to educational institutions (like student uniforms) etc.,

The Jupiter

Sky blue, yellow, golden shades, traditional dresses, religious and functional costumes, dresses for the auspicious and festive occasions, neat and clean dresses. Dresses that will add piousness and prestige to the owner. Respectable and admirable dresses belong to the Jupiter.

The Venus

Costly costumes, shining bright ones, silky materials, dresses that add glory and glamour to the wearer. Rich and royal costumes are indicated by the Venus.

The Saturn

The royal blue, navy blue, black, darker shades of all colours, old dresses, worn out and torn out clothes, dresses low in quality and price, foul smelling ones.

The Rahu

The violet and dark blue coloured costumes, broad striped and big checked designs, shiny costumes like that of a snake, oversized dresses, too much of dressing, gaudy in colours and style.

The Ketu

Small checks and very narrow striped patterns, dresses of spiritual leaders, dresses which are connected with religious ceremonies and occasions, saintly costumes, shiny colours and clothes, under sized garments, dusty clothes, inadequate and incomplete dresses.

The colours represented by the Mercury will be mild and pleasant like that of the colours of the Jupiter. The colours signified by the Venus are glittering and shiny similar to that of the colours of the Rahu.

Applications of the Jamakkol Prasanam

Preparation of the Jamakkol Prasanam Chart

Now we have learnt how to calculate the Udhaya, the Aaruda, the Kavippu and also how to write the Jama graha (the planets in the outside). We will work out some examples to draw this Jamakkol chart before proceeding to the actual predictions. Yes, we would be using the Software to construct the Jamakkol charts in our day to day practice. One such easy and user friendly Jamakkol software is available with us for precise calculations and predictions. But, we must also learn how to prepare the Jamakkol chart manually. This will help us to cross check the computer prepared chart. And it will come handy at times where the computer is not available. And it will also increase our competence level in the Jamakkol prasanam. So it is always suggested to get manually trained to prepare the Jamakkol charts at the initial stages for the better understanding of the concepts involved.

Example 1

05/01/2019, 11 49 a.m., Thanjavur.

Step 1. Calculation of the Aarudam.

Now the time of the prasanam is 11 49. To find out the Aarudam we need only the minutes. So we remove the hour 11 and took only the minute's value 49. We allocated five minutes to each rasi from the Mesha and proceed with the next signs. Thus the time 49 falls in the Makara rasi. This time refers to the Makara rasi when allocating five minutes to each rasi. The minute's value 49 means that the Aarudam is in the 10th house, the Makara.

Step 2. Calculation of the Udhayam.

Now the procedure for the calculation of the Udhayam is done as follows.

The Sun rise on that day was at 6 35 am in Thanjavur.

H min

The time of the Prasanam 11 49

The time of Sunrise 06 35

Subtracting 05 14

Converting this in to minutes (05 X 60) + 14   314 minutes.

To convert this into degrees, divide it by 2 ...314/2 = 157 degrees
                                                            00 minutes.

Now add this with the degree of the transit Sun on 05/01/2019
                                            260 degrees 29 minutes.

(This value can be obtained from any good almanac)

Adding .... 417 degrees 31 minutes.

Since the value has exceeded the 360 degrees, we are subtracting 360 from 417 degrees and 31 minutes. It is now 417 31 − 360 00 = 057 31 degrees.

This degree falls in the sign Taurus in the star of the Margasira second pada. So the Udhaya lagna is Mithuna and the Udhaya lagna star is the Margasira.

Step 3. Calculation of the Kavippu.

To find out the Kavippu, we must first identify the Veedhi in which the transit Sun is moving at that time. Here the Sun is in the sign of Dhanus during its monthly routine transits. Since the Sun is transiting in the sign of Dhanus, the Veedhi is Mithuna Veedhi. So now count from the Aarudam to the Mithuna rasi. The Aarudam is Makara. While we count from the Makara to the Mithuna it comes 6. Now count 6 from the Udhaya lagna and put the Kavippu there. The Udhaya has been identified as the Meena. The 6th sign from it is the Simha. Hence the Kavippu is now in the sign of Simha. We will now prepare the Jamakkol chart for this.

Step 4. The Jamakkol configuration.

		Udhayam	Veedhi
		05/01/2019, 11 47 am., Thanjavur	
Aaruda			
Transit Sun	Kavippu		

Kaarakathuvams

We have been doing it consciously as a practice to give importance and prominent coverage to the Kaarakathuvas in every one of our books. In astrology, there are many systems practiced and each and every method has its own individual rules and approach. They all revolve round the 9 planets, 12 signs and the 27 stars only. Interestingly, it is found that the Kaarakathuvas of the above three entities remain almost the same in the various astrological techniques and they are widely used in all those systems.

The study of the Kaarakathuvas might look like a primary education for some. But, if it is viewed it in the other way, they are the basics and the fundamental blocks and also clues to the astrological predictions. The correct identification of the Kaaraka gives the exact results. Suppose, in a chart we find the 2nd bhava is getting affected in a Medical astrology case study. Now which one it will affect, the sight or the speech? The answer is not simple. But now if the Kaarakathuvas are known accurately the solution can be made. If the 2nd bhava or its lord is connected to the illuminating planets, the Sun, the Moon or the Venus, the vision in the eye will get affected. If it is the Mercury, the speech will be disturbed. If it is the Mars, the teeth will become troublesome. This is how and where the kaarakathuvas are applied differently to arrive at the precise predictions. We are taking utmost care to update, redefine and replenish the information on the Kaarakathuvas in not only in all our new books, but also in the all the subsequent editions and reprints of our older books also.

There is an inestimable number of living and non-living things in this world. In astrology we correlate them to the nine planets, the twelve Rasis and the twelve Bhavas and call them as the Kaarakathuvas or the Significators. All the things available in this world are allotted to a planet or to a rasi or to a bhava and those things are referred as the kaarakathuvas of that particular entity it has been assigned to. It is no less than a human effort to memorise all the significators available. But if we understand the fundamentals involved in the rationale of the kaarakathuvas classification, it would be a great assistance in prediction.

The people, the places, the characteristics, the behaviour, the animals, the birds, the plants, the professions, the five natural elements, the countries, the relations, the diseases, the natural events, the metals, the food varieties, the parts of body, the activities etc., and thus all the living and the non-living have been classified as kaarakathuvas. They are either related to a planet, or to a rasi or to a bhava and then the kaarakathuvas are identified with a particular entity. Even though one kaarakathuvam is assigned to a particular planet the influence of all the other planets also can be seen associated to that kaarakathuvas.

The allocation of kaarakathuvas and the segmentation of the characteristics and functional attributes for various planets have a distinguishing and vital purpose. They are primarily designed to be useful in the astrological prediction. Instead of describing that the particular planets would confer these qualities or properties, the astute astrological pioneers have given those attributes to the planets themselves. They have not told that a well-placed Sun would give authority, but instead they have earmarked the Sun for the power and the authority. Similarly, the Moon represented the Motherhood and the emotions; the Mars personified the adventurous and the commanding spirit; the Mercury symbolised the intelligence and the communication; the Jupiter stood for the auspiciousness and the uprightness; the Venus denoted the beauty and the luxury; the Saturn indicated the slow and the laziness; the shadow planets the Rahu and the Ketu were recognised for all the clandestine activities. The planets themselves do not carry the qualities, but, they bestow these feature on the natives. The attributes are postulated to be the characteristics of the different planets and named as the Kaarakathuvas. The planetary influences on the native are thus symbolically represented by the kaarakathuvas. And consequently the traits of the native can be realised using the information of the kaarakathuvas. The personification or the figurative representations of the Kaarakathuvas was an ingenious way of remembering the planetary effects.

The kaarakathuvam concerned with the query should be first identified by the astrologer and then depending on the status of the kaaraka planet or the kaaraka bhava the question is dealt with. For a question related to the marriage, the kaaraka planets are the Mars and the Venus. The answer is arrived after studying the position of the Mars and the Venus and combination or aspect of the other planets with these two planets the Mars and the Venus. At the same time the position of the Seventh house and its lord are also ascertained, as the seventh house is the Kalasthrasthana. Thus the Bhava and the Kaaraka go hand in hand in arriving at the astrological predictions.

1. Graha Kaarakathuvams

The word Graha is commonly used to describe the planets. But it refers to the all the celestial bodies, according to the astrological savant late Shri B.V. Raman. One of the meanings of the word graha is "to absorb" and since the planets absorbs the light from the Sun, this meaning is opt. The Graha also means "to attract", which indicates the gravitational pull of those heavenly structures. According to the Greek astrology, the origin of the word planet is from the Greek word *the Planetai,* which means the wanderer or the traveller because of their apparent motion in the sky.

The planets we refer here in astrology are the nine planets in the solar system which include the Sun and the Moon besides the shadowy planets the Rahu and the Ketu. The astrology is the study of the movements, the positions and the conjunctions of the Sun, the Moon and the other seven planets and also the stars and how they affect the lives and the character of the living beings in the earth. The important kaarakathuvam of each and every of this nine planets are discussed here. How they are correlated to the astrological predictions is also explained.

THE SUN

GENERAL

The Sun or the Surya is the center of all the astrological principles. All the planets revolve round the Sun at different elliptical orbits with varying speed and periodicity. In astronomy the Sun is a Star and in the astrology the Sun in is considered as the Star-Planet. The mean distance of the Sun from the Earth is approximately 14.96 crore kilometers. The Sunlight reaches us in eight minutes and nineteen seconds. The Sun rules over the sign Simha and the stars Karthikai, Uthra phalguni and Uthrashada. The dasa period of the Sun is 6 years. The Sun travels approximately one degree per day. It takes roughly 3 days and 6 hours and 35 minutes to transverse a star pada and about 13 days to cover a star. The Sun is responsible for the change of seasons.

The Sun is the center of the Solar system and all the planets revolve around it. So the Sun is like the leader of the System. Similarly, the leaders or the heads in a family or in an organization or in a department is symbolised by the Sun. Therefore, the Sun denotes the father, who is the head of the family. The Sun denotes the Kings, the Rulers, the administrative heads, the politicians etc., in the same way. The Sun represents the Presidents, the Prime ministers and the Chief Ministers. Any person in the superior ranks of all the professions is indicated by the Sun. The Sun represents the light and the energy. The Sun denotes the valour. Come what may, the Sun rises in the East in the morning and sets in the West in the evening and therefore the Sun denotes the punctuality. Similarly, the Sun operates on its own and other planets revolve around it. The native also like to act according to his free will and he does not like or abide by any control. The Sun does not wait for anything to raise, sail or set. Similarly, the body parts which are involuntary in function like the heart are represented by the Sun.

The Sun denotes enormous energy and the power. Thus the Sun represents the stamina and the valour. The Sun is the planet for imagination. In whichever bhava the Sun is placed, the native will have fantastic and wild imaginations concerned with the bhava. Suppose the Sun is in the 7th house, the native will have fanciful dreams and expectations about his /her life partner. In the 10th house, it will give amazing plans and insights about his/her profession.

The Sun is the planet of light and so it denotes the Eyes. The other planet which denotes the eyes is the illuminating planet the Moon. The Venus which is also connected with the bright light indicates the eyes, but it denotes the one eyed persons. Because according to the Hindu mythology, the Sukracharya is the one eyed Guru of the Asuras.

The Sun gives not only the heat but also the illumination. So in the Dasa of the planet Sun or the planet which is going to touch the Sun next or the planet which is placed in the star of the Sun, will make the native popular and throw him in the lime light of publicity and fame.

The Sun sets in the West. The signs of the Gemini, the Libra and the Aquarius denote the direction of the West. Therefore, the Sun looses its power when placed in those signs. The Sun is debilitated in the house of the Libra. So the Libra natives have to be careful with the Kaarakathuvas of the Sun. They should avoid climbing mountains. They should not sit in the upstairs and take important decisions. Because the Sun represents the upstairs and the elevated places. Similarly, the Libra person should not opt for opening of the head for any treatment and instead try to treat with alternatives like medicines. The Sun gives life to the Earth without expecting anything. When two or three planets are placed in the stars of the Sun in a horoscope, the native will be liberal in nature. The Sun denotes both the Power, pride and also the generosity.

The Sun represents the encroaching. The King used to trespass into others freedom, territory, the property, their Rights, land or even in their family. When the Sun is adversely placed in the chart in the 2nd and the 7th houses and further gets malefic influence, the native tends to live with other's wife or husband.

The Sun is surrounded by the other 8 planets and the cascade of millions of stars. So the persons born with the positive influence of the Sun, the Simha rasi or the Simha lagna or in the stars of the Sun, usually belong to a large and well known families. They also like to live as a joint family.

Ability, abnormal, adamancy, administration, administrators, advanced ideas, aerodromes, aero planes, airport, alarm, alchemy, anarchy, anger, antiques, altruism, astringent taste, astronomy, authority, aviation, battery, boldness, boycotts, bravery, bright, brilliance, captaincy, celebrities, charity, coarse cloth, commanding personality, compassionate, consciousness, confidence, conscience, courage, daytime, determination, dignity, divorce, dominance, dynamo, earth quake, eastern direction, eccentric, ego, electricity, exile, fame, famous personalities, Father, fire, firmness, fond of hot food, foreign, forests, formal dresses, freedom, gaudy, generous, governance, Government, governmental favour, government jobs, graceful, happiness, heat, helicopter, honesty, honour, hopes, hunting, hurricanes, immunity, independent, individuality, influential, intelligence, invention, King, kingdom, Kshatriya, leadership, liberation, liberal attitude, lightning, lion, lordship, Lord Shiva, lord of the daytime, majestic, magnanimous, masculine, medical education, medicine, merciful, modern, mountains, pardoning propensity, paternal matters, penance, perseverance, personality, politics, power, prestige, pride, prominence, Rajo guna, regal, regalia, reliability, religious leaders, reputation, the Royalty, sacrifice, Sanskrit and Telugu languages, Saivite philosophy, Science, scientists, sea, self-confidence, self-reliance, self-respect, severity, Soul, spiritual powers, steady, strictness, strikers, summer season, superiority, Sunday, sympathy, tiger, trustworthiness, utility of fire, victory over enemies, virtuous traits, valour, victory in battles, vigour, vitality, wickedness, will power, wood, woolen clothes.

BODY PARTS AND DISEASES

The abdomen, arteries, baldness, big toe, bile, body temperature, bones, head, heart, right eye, sparse hair, spinal cord, stomach, yellowish eyes are the main body parts denoted by the Sun.

The bone disorder, diseases involving the Pitha, diseases related to very high body temperature, epilepsy, eye diseases, fainting, headache, heart ailments, hemorrhage, meningitis, mental disorder, migraine, myopia and hyperopia (short sightedness and long sightedness), pains, palpitations, rheumatic diseases, sunstroke, syncope, throat disorders, typhoid are notable diseases represented by the Sun.

OBJECTS

All articles that are circular in shape, almonds, asafetida, bishops' weed, cardamom, camphor, crimson colour, chillies, copper, dazzling objects, diamond, electricity, elephant, gold, gold ornaments, groundnut, hard core trees, herbal medicines, ivory, medicines, neat and well creased dresses, orange colour, onions, pepper, platinum, radar, radium, red colour, red lotus flower, rice, ruby, television, wheat, wool are some of the objects represented by the Sun.

PLACES

The buildings or the houses which provide permanent income, Capital cities, dry and hot places, dwelling in the forest, forts, hilly terrain, jungles, jewelry shops, lodges, mansions, mountains, multi storied buildings, outer corridor, palaces, public buildings, shamiana, shopping complexes, Siva temples, Sourashtra country, thatched roof, top storey of the buildings.

PROFESSION

The Sun is the head of the family of the planets. Therefore, the Sun indicates the family professions and also profession with large central administrative structure surrounded by number of branches. Administration, all jobs in the Government, all jobs of permanent nature and secured income, all politicians and posts like the M.P., the M.L.A., and similar posts up to the level of the Corporation, the Municipalities, the Taluk and the village panchayats belong to the Sun. The business dealing with the gold, the ornaments and the precious stones, department heads, directors, doctors especially those belong to the allopathy system, goldsmith, gold gilding, jobs in Public Undertakings, judges, Heads of the educational institutions like the schools, the colleges, the Universities etc., the managers, the pawn brokers, professions connected with the fuel, professions and business running through ones' generations, supervisory work, team leaders.

GOVERNMENT

The Government in all the terms and senses is referred only by the Sun. The Government officials of higher hierarchy, the administrators of the Country or the State or any place or region right from the Kings, the Queens, the Presidents, the Prime Ministers, the Governors, the Chief Ministers, the Ministers, the Mayors, the Collectors etc., are denoted by the Sun. the money lenders and receivers of the money on behalf of the Government, the people wielding the authority, the people in the command, people who work in increasing and accumulating the Government revenue, the Heads of Departments, the people responsible to control the crimes and also the measures undertook by them including the punishments levied, Magistrates are some of the other professions indicated by the Sun.

RELATIONS

Father, father in law (after marriage), eldest son, religious and spiritual leaders.

RELIGION

Worshipping the Soul, the Sun, Lord Shiva, the Fire or the Light is indicated. Normally they like to worship the Nature.

THE MOON

GENERAL

The Moon or the Chandra is a satellite of the earth and in astrology it is considered as one among the planets. The Moon is the fastest of all the planets and transits a sign in about two and a half days and covers the entire zodiac in about 27 days. The Moon is at a distance of about 3.9 lakh kilometers from our Earth. The movement of the Moon around the earth causes the day and the nights. The Moon does not have a light of its own and it reflects the light of the Sun. When the Moon is powerfully placed in a native's horoscope, he would also assume the quality of absorbing the influence of other persons and situations and act accordingly. The Moon is termed as a feminine planet and as such possesses the womanly proclivity. The Moon has a watery nature. In Indian astrology the sign in which the Moon is placed in the natal horoscope is a very significant factor and it is called as the Janma rasi or the Chandra Lagna. The predictions are done based on the Janma rasi also in the Indian context. The Moon rules the sign Cancer and gets exalted in the Taurus and faces its fall in the Scorpio. The Moon rules over the stars of the Rohini, the Hasta and the Sravana. The dasa period of the Moon is 10 years. The Moon transits 12 degrees and 41 minutes and 55 seconds in a day. It takes approximately 30 hours to transverse a sign and about 27 days to cover the complete zodiac circle. In astronomy, the Moon takes about 27.32 days to complete one revolution period.

The Moon is the ruler of the 4th house of the Kaala Purusha. The Moon denotes the swift movements and also called as the planet for the travels. Any planet which touches the Moon is fond of travelling. Suppose, the Sun moves towards the Moon. It will indicate that the father of the native is a frequent traveller. The Moon denotes the beauty. In whichever bhava the Moon is placed, the person represented by that Kaaraka will be beautiful. For example, when the Moon is in the 4th bhava, the mother will be good-looking.

The Kaaraka person represented by the Moon, will have motherly qualities. Suppose, the Moon is in the 9th house. Then the father will have motherly affection and attitude. If it is in the 11th house, the elder brother or the friend will have maternal affection towards the native.

The Moon represents the woman who are either pregnant or the mother with the child. This information can be useful in situations like this. Suppose a man wants to go in for a second marriage. The 2nd marriage is denoted by the 9th house. If the 9th bhava adhipathi is posted in the stars of the Moon, the person will marry a woman who is with a child or a pregnant lady.

The Moon has no light of its own and it receives and reflects the light from the Sun. Similarly, the person with the karaka influence of the Moon will depend on someone else for their survival. Likewise, being the Moon a reflecting planet, the natives with the influence of the Moon will reflect the words and the feelings of others and the situations. For example, these are the persons who will shed tears on seeing emotional scenes in a cinema theatre.

The Moon has two phases waxing and waning. The waning means decrease or depreciation. So when the waning Moon is placed in the 4th place, the properties of the native will place devaluation. As the 4th bhava represents the Mother, the relationship with the mother side will face depreciation or the number of relatives in the mother side will be in the declining mode.

The Moon is a watery planet and further it owns the watery house, the Cancer. The afflicted Moon would be responsible for the dangers from the water. The occurrence of the death due to drowning in water is an extreme situation. But, even the falling down in watery places, the vehicles got stuck in the water, the sinus troubles, the exposure to even a mild cold or slight shower will bring about health problems, the rainy season brings ill health, getting allergic to water in the new and unfamiliar places, etc., are some of the water sensitive problems for these natives.

The absentmindedness, absorption, accidents in water, activities that would give dishonour and bad name, the amusements, anxiety, aquatic creatures, aquatic matters, artistic form, artistic objects, attractiveness, auspiciousness, awareness, bad conduct, beauty, Brand names, branding, brilliance, bulky body, charm, change of places like residences, cheating mentality, cheese, child birth, coolness, conception, consciousness, deceitfulness, delivery, depreciation, deterioration, devotion, digestion, distant travels, doubtful, eating food, emotions, emotional nature, evil character, fame, fantasy, feeding, females, fertility, fickle mindedness, fluctuations in life, food, frankness, freebies, generosity, handsome, hasty, higher levels of consciousness, human nature, identity, illegal contacts, imagination, impregnation, indecisiveness, independent, infancy, influential, ingenious, journeys, kindness, knowledge, lakes, laziness, liquid diet, liquid substances, loss of memory, lungs, lustrous face and the shining body, maternity, Mind, mental agitation, memory power, metamorphosis, modesty, moist, mood swings, Mother, motherhood, motherly nature, mild, music, navigation, nomadic life, north western direction, notoriety, nourishment, novel, nurse, nursing care, omens, opinions, outstanding identity, paleness, phlegmatic nature, physical growth, pious, polite, popularity, pre-adult stage, pregnancy, prominence, prone to frequent changes, queens, rain, realization, reflective tendency, rivers, royal favour, salty taste, Sathwa guna, sea, sensitive, serenity, shining, short stature, shyness, sleep, softness, stomach disorders, suspicious mind, sweets, sweet disposition, sweet fragrance, swift, Tamil language, tenderness, theft, thief, timid, Titles, tolerance, tranquility, tricks, tricky nature, trustless, vacillation, vagabond, vegetation, wavering of the mind, watery grave, wear and tear, whiteness, white coloured cloth, white lily flower, white feathered birds, women's associations, wrong doings

All that are experienced by the body and/or the mind are indicated by the Moon only.

BODY PARTS

The abdomen, the alimentary canal, the blood, the blood circulation, the breasts, the breast milk, the brain, the chest, the consciousness, the intestine, the kidneys, the left eye for the men and the right eye for the women, the lungs, the lymphatic system, the ovaries, the physical body as well as the inner soul, the renal system, the saliva, the stomach, the urinary bladder, the uterus, the watery content of the body, the womb are the body parts indicated by the Moon.

DISEASES

The diseases associated with the Moon are the alcoholism, anemia, asthma, Beriberi (lack of Vitamin B), blood disorders, bronchitis, colic pains, common cold, cough, debility, diarrhea, diseases of the glands, dropsy, dyspepsia, dysentery, effusions in the body, eosinophilia, epilepsy, eye diseases, fever with chills and rigor, gastric ulcer, hydrocele, hypertension, hysteria, insanity, jaundice, laziness, leuco-derma, loss of vitality, lunacy, malfunctioning of the uterus, sense of memory as well as loss of memory, menses, menstrual problems, nausea, nervous disability, phlegmatic disorders, pleurisy, rundown conditions, stroke, tastelessness, throat disorders, tuberculosis, typhoid, urinary disorders, unconsciousness, varicose veins, vertigo, vomiting, worm infestations.

OBJECTS

The objects and things which are to be consumed fresh on a daily basis which otherwise may go rotten and get decayed are the Kaaraka of the Moon. The examples are the milk, the vegetables, the flowers, the fruits etc., to name a few. Generally, all the commodities related to the foodstuff and all the jobs or the occupations connected with the food items are represented by the Moon (the hotels, the fast food joints, canteens, catering service and cafe).

All things that are moving fast, aluminum, bell metal, betel leaves, bottles, bulls, butter, camphor, canals, conch shell, candles, clouds, cotton, cotton plant, cows, crab, crystals, cucumber, curd, dams, ducks, eggs, fans, fine cloth, flowers, fruits, garments, ghee, glass, grocery items, honey, horses, ivory, jowar, juices, mammals, milk, milk products, milky juice of plants, movements, mushrooms, new dresses, oysters, paddy, pearls, pearl studded ornaments, plants, plantains, poultry, rice, saffron, salt, sea, sea produce, ships, shopping, silver, snakes, sugar, sugarcane, sumptuous meal, taverns, tea leaves, tear drops, tender leaves, tortoise, transfer from one place to another, umbrellas, vegetables and fruits having a high water content, wandering here and there, washing machines, washed clothes, water heater, wet, wheat, white colour and white coloured objects, yachts are few of the objects denoted by the Moon.

PLACES

Agricultural fields, aquarium, bathing Ghats, bath rooms, bath tubs, bed room, fountains, gardens, the herbarium, kitchen sinks, lakes, north western direction, ocean, places where women stay, plant nursery, plumbing stations, ponds, rivers, riverside, sea, swimming pools, watery places and washing areas are denoted by the Moon.

PROFESSION

Advertising, agriculture, cooks, dairy (milk) farm, export business, fertilizer mart, grocery shop, horticulture, laundry and dry cleaning, liquid substances, liquor shop, magician, marketing, Navy, newspaper mart, nurses, sailor, sales personnel, seamen, trading of beverages, coconut, cool drinks, coral, fish, food stuff, fruits, milk and milk products, paddy, pearls, public related jobs like the bus conductors and ration shop wallahs, rice, salt, spices and vegetables, water related jobs like water supply, mineral water, water purifier etc.,

RELATIONS

Elderly women, elder sister, general public, Mother, mother in law (after marriage), persons interacting with the general public (bus conductor, sales persons etc.), persons giving away freebies, persons who use the word "always" frequently, public works department and the staff.

Well placed Moon denotes poets, writers, imagination and fantasy and if Moon is afflicted, then it symbolises the mentally deranged persons.

RELIGION

The goddess Parvathi and all female goddesses are represented by the Moon especially those which are without much adornment.

THE MARS

GENERAL

The Mars or the Kuja or the Chevvai is the planet next to our earth in the solar orbit. The Mars has close resemblances with the earth and the Indian astrology says that the Mars is the son of the Earth (Bhoomi Sudha). In the Western astrology, the Mars is the name of the Roman god of war. In Indian mythology also the Chevvai is associated with the Lord Muruga who is said to be the Divine Commander. The Mars is bright reddish orange in colour. The Mars is at an average distance of about 22.79 crore kilometers from the Sun. The Mars travels around the Sun once in every 687 Earth days. The Kuja rules the signs of Mesha and the Virschika and the stars Margasira, Chitra and Dhanishta. It is exalted in Makara and gets debilitated in Kataka. The Mars dasa rules for a period of 7 years. The Mars took 5 days to travel one pada of a star. It takes about 45 days to travel through a rasi. The Martian day is about 24 hours and 40 minutes long.

The Mars has the ownership of the Mesha and the Virschika and these two rasis are the 1st and the 8th of the Kaala Purusha. The first house or the Lagna denotes the birth and the 8th house denotes the longevity.

So the Mars is the planet which is travelling throughout the life of the people.

The Mars is the planet for the protection and the security. So the organs which serve as a protective cover in the human body are denoted by the Mars. The skull which protects the brain, the eye brows and the eyelids which cover the eyes, the teeth which shields the tongue, the bones which protect the internal organs and the body structure are all denoted by the Mars only. Not only that, the brother who is supposed to protect the sisters, the husband who is protecting the wife, the police which is protecting the society, the army which is defending the Nation, etc., are all the kaarakathuvas of the Mars. The compound wall, the fence around the house or the landed property, the main door of the building, the locks etc., which protect the house are all denoted by the Mars. Interestingly, the dogs which are known for their security in houses and other places are represented by the Mars only. Similarly, the Mars is the planet for the self defence martial arts like the Boxing, the Judo, the Karate, the Silambham (fighting with the canes) etc., And also the coaches or the instructors of these kinds of sports are also denoted by the Mars only. The Mars is the kaaraka planet for all types of weapons. And whichever God is found carrying a weapon in his/her hands is the kaaraka of the Mars. For example, the Lord Muruga carries a sharp instrument called the Vel (a spear like weapon) and the Lord Hanuman holds a Gadai (a mace like weapon) to name a few.

The ability to fulfill tasks, abortions, abrasions, administrative ability, accidents, action, activity, acumen in warfare, adamant, adventure, ambition, anger, argumentative, armed forces, assassins, athletes, bravery, breakages, bites, boldness, boxing, boxer, brawls, cannon, career in army, challenges, chivalry, combat, combustion, commander, competitions, competitors, competitive spirit, competitive sports, conflicts, courage, cruelty, curfew, daring, defensive skills, defensive techniques, determination, dexterity, dictatorship, diseases, disputes, drivers, eagles, ego, emergencies, endurance, enemies, enmity, energy, engineering, excessive lust, extremism, extremists, fearless, fevers, fights, fire, firemen, fleshy, fury, gymnastics, harsh speech, haste, hot and spicy food, hunting dogs, inflammation, injury, Kshatriya caste, landed assets, Lord Muruga, Lord Narasimha, lust, manliness, martial arts, masculinity, masters who teach self-defense arts like Karate, Judo etc., mason and other workers involved in the construction jobs, medium height, militant, military, non-systematic, non-believing, obstinacy, operations, organising capacity, passionate, patrol, perseverance, police, power-hungry, pride, quarrels, quarrelsome, rape, rebels, rebellion, resourceful, revolution, revengeful, robust, rude, rash and rough behaviour, scarlet colour, scars, security, self-confidence, self-dependency, servitude, short tempered nature, sports persons, sports grounds, stadium, stamina, strenuous, strength, strong, surgery, tenacity, Thamo guna, thoughtlessness, torture, toughness, uniformed services, unnatural and unlawful sexual tendencies and behaviour (if Mars is afflicted), valour, valiant, vigour, violence, violent acts and temperament, volcano, vultures, wars, warlike situations, warrior, welding, well-built physique, withstanding capacity, wrestling, wrestler, zealous activities, zealous temperament.

Most of the Kaarakathuvas of the Mars are similar to that of the Sun's Kaarakathuvas. But the difference lies in the fact that the Sun has the Kingly qualities and royal touch, while the Mars has a drape of certain amount of rash and roughness.

BODY PARTS AND DISEASES

The blood, bones, bone narrow, eye lids, forehead, hemoglobin, left ear, muscular system, menstrual cycle, menstrual system, nails, nose, pimples, rigid muscles, small pox, stamina, strength, teeth, twirled mustache, valour, virility are denoted by the Mars.

The diseases which are associated with the Mars are the abortions, abscesses, bile disorder, bleeding disorder, blood disorders, boils, burns, carbuncle, chicken pox, complications of elevated body temperature, cuts, diseases of the spleen, fevers, Filaria, firefighting kits, fire engine, fractures, furnaces, gall stones, headache, hemorrhage, hernia, high blood pressure, head injuries, hot eruptions, inflammations, injury, injury or death due to fire or accidents or by violent means, measles, meningitis, pimples, plague, ruptures, scars on the head or face, shooting pain, small pox, tooth-ache, tumours, typhoid, wounds.

OBJECTS

Acids, arecanut, all types of machinery and their parts, arms and ammunitions, axe, beams, bow and arrow, cannon, cashew nuts, chemicals, cigarettes, copper, coriander seeds, coral, coral ornaments, dogs, dried vegetation, drugs, electrical and electronic household appliances, explosives, fire, garlic, ginger, gold, goods carrier, groundnut, heavy gadgets, heavy vehicles, horns, iron, jaggery, jowar, knives, land, liquor, medicines, metals, minerals, mustard, needles, ovens, pillars, pottery, power generators, radiators, razors, red color, red coloured garments, red chili, reddish flowers, red gram, red wood, saw, scissors, sharp edged weapons, sheep, steel, sword, tamarind, thorny plants, tigers, triangular shaped objects, tobacco, urad dhal, weapons of all kind wheat, wolf.

PLACES

Army units, army bases, army training centers, brick kiln, building sites, factories, firecracker units, furnaces, gymnasium, hiding places of thieves, hospitals, houses, kitchen, lime kiln, meat shops, mines, mortuary, operation theatres, ovens, pillars, places full of thorny bushes, places where explosions took place, places where accidents frequently happen, places where fire broke out, police stations, research laboratories, slaughter houses, southern direction, training centers, vast areas of agricultural lands, warfront, work-shops.

PROFESSION

The adventurous activities like the mountaineering, agriculture, all the work related to machines, army chief, army commander, barbers, blacksmiths, brokers, building constructors, butchers, carpenters, chemists, cooks, dentists, dyeing units, engineers, fertilizer merchants, fire service personnel, forest department, industries connected with the fire, jobs connected with knives, metals, sharp edged objects and red coloured substances like bricks, blood, chilies etc., managers, masons, mechanics, medical shops, metallurgist, persons in the security and protective services like police, military, security guards, potters, soldiers and watch men, professions related to coral, copper, knives etc., real estate dealers, sportspersons, stone crushing, stone quarry, supervisor, surgeons, surveyor, tailors, tanning of leather, trainer in gym and exercise halls, watch repair, weapons manufacturer, etc., are represented by the Mars.

RELATIONS

In a male's horoscope the Mars denotes the co born and in the female's horoscope the Mars signifies her husband in addition to her co born. The younger co born and brother in law for both the husband and the wife are indicated by the Mars.

RELIGION

The Mars denotes Lord Muruga in the masculine houses and the deity Durga Devi in the feminine houses. The deities symbolizing great fury (Lord Narasimha, Bhadra Kaali) and those in the combative posture.

THE MERCURY

GENERAL

The Mercury or the Bhudha is the smallest of all the planets and closest to the Sun. It has a diameter of about 4,879 kilometers which is about two fifths of the Earth's diameter. The name Mercury was given by the ancient Romans in honour of the swift messenger of their gods. The Bhudha goes around the Sun in 88 Earth days. The Bhudha always remain within 28 degrees from the Sun. The Bhudha rules over the stars Aslesha, Jyeshta and Revathi and the dual signs the Mithuna and the Kanya. The Bhudha is exalted at the Kanya and gets debilitated in the Meena. The dasa period is 17 years. In Indian astrology, the Bhudha is considered to be the son of Moon. The Bhudha becomes a benefic when he is alone and when he is in the association of benefic planets. The Bhudha becomes a malefic in the company of malefic planets. The Mercury takes 3 days and 10 hours to cover one Nakshtra pada and about 30 days to transit a rasi. It goes retrograde once in 3 months for a period of 21 days. The combustion period is 22 days. The Mercury takes 59 Earth days to rotate once in its axis. As a result, the duration of one-day time in Mercury is equal to the 176 Earth days.

The Mercury is in a way the most cordial planet. It is called as Sowmya, the peace loving. The Bhudha is the Kaaraka for the speech. But we can observe that the stars of the Mercury, the Aslesha, the Jyeshta and the Revathi are located in the houses of Mute signs. In English also, the well conducted oration is called as the Mercurial speech. At the same time, Mercurian temperament describes fickle and inconstant nature. So both are true with the Mercury, the intelligence and the rapidly changing behaviour. The houses Gemini and the Virgo come under the classification of the Common houses and the Mercury is also classified as having the dual nature.

The Mercury is the planet connected with the planning, thinking, grasping, listening, observing etc. These are all the essential ingredients of Intelligence and knowledgeable. The Mercury is classified as the kaaraka for the communication. So all forms of the communications, the communication aids, the communication services, the communicators like the radio and television announcers, the news readers, the anchors, the Jockeys, the reporters, the commentators, the critics, etc., belong to the Bhudha. The speech, the documents, the records, the newspapers, the magazines, the letters, the postal service, the courier organisations, the mail, the message, the telegram, the photostat copies, the ambassadors, the agents, the middlemen, the brokers, the Registrar, the lawyers, the broadcasters, the announcements, the advertising, the posters and all these type of objects which communicate some message or information are classified as the Kaaraka of the Mercury. The chief communicating accessory, the tongue is denoted by the Mercury.

The documents like the ration card, PAN card, the Aadhar card, the driving license, the Identification card, the name badge, the address, the door number, the passbook, the cheque book, the Passport, the educational certificates, the text books, the black boards and the sign boards are some more of the kaarakathuvas of the Mercury. All these are identifying aids to recognise a person. The Name which is the main identifying symbol for anyone is also the Kaaraka of the Mercury. The documents are represented by the Mercury and also by the Jupiter. The difference is the document paper and the written document are represented by the Mercury. Once the document is completed with all the necessary formalities and gets the proper sign and seal of the authorities and thereby the legal procedures are sanctioned, then the document becomes the Jupiter.

The accounts, accountancy, accountants, advertisement, agents, agreements, ambassador, ambivalent, analytical, arithmetic, astrology, astronomy, attraction, auditing, bargain, bills, biographies, birds, boards, bribery, broker, bulletins, business acumen, cables, cajolery, catalogues, certificates, chanting the Mantras, child, clerks, commerce, communication of all types, communication channels, communication aids, communication agencies, communicating techniques, communicators, committee, compromise, correspondence, cowardice, critic, couriers agents, cunningness, damsels, data, delivery, dexterity, diplomacy, discriminative, documents, double speech, dual nature, dual acts, education, electronic gadgets, eloquence, epics, eunuch, facts, fluency, friendship, friends, frequent short travels, funny acts, funny speech, gentleness, gossips, grammar, graphology, hand writing, impartiality, indecisive, information, installments, instructions, intelligence, investigation, journalists, jovial, jugglery, knowledge, language, learning, literature, logical, manuscripts, mathematics, mediator, mentality, memory, message, messengers, methodical, middle-men, morning time, multi-linguist, multi-tasking, name change, nephew, NEWS, numbers, numerology, oratory skills, oscillations, paintings, partnership, pens, pick pockets, plans, planning, pleasant, presence of mind, prince, princely life, print media, proverbs, prudent nature, puns, quick grasping power, quick wit, quotations, Rajo guna, the reasoning ability, records, recording, repetition, repetitive acts, reports, rumours, sarcasm, satellite network, scholars, scientific instruments, secretaries, senses, sense of humour, sharp intellect, shrewdness, speech, stories, tactical, talent to recall, tall stature, telegrams, the Telugu language, trade and commercial activities, traders, translations, unsteadiness, vacillations, virgin, versatility, vocabulary, volatile, the Vysya caste, walking, wind, words, writer, writing, writing instruments, writing style, written scripts, wit, young age, youth.

BODY PARTS AND DISEASES

The arms, the fingers, feet, the forehead, the hands, the larynx, the lungs, the neck, the nervous system, the nostrils, the palms, the shoulders, the skin, the throat, the tongue and the valves of the heart are the major organs represented by the Mercury. The nerves represented by the Mercury are medium sized ones. The fin capillary like nerves which are situated in the parts like the brain are represented by the Ketu.

The diseases such as the apoplexy, convulsions, deafness, dumbness, ear ailments, forgetfulness, gout, impotency, leukoderma, loss of sensation, mental aberrations, nasal disorders, nervous breakdown, neuralgia, skin diseases of all types including the leprosy, speech disorders, stammering, sweating in excess, tremors of the hands and vertigo are indicated by the Mercury.

OBJECTS

Any object signifying education and knowledge belongs to the Mercury (who is known as the Vidya kaaraka). All varieties of edible fruits and vegetables, Atlas book of Maps and charts, Bank passbooks, black boards, bicycle, birds, bell metal, brand names, brass, brochures, budding plants, catalogues, cats, calendar, chameleon, codes, copiers, copy writing, diagrams, diary, dictionary, directory, dust, emerald, e mails, fax messages, files, green gram, green colour, horses, identity cards, keys, leaves, ledgers, magnifying glasses, Mercury, mobile phones, name badges, papers, passports, pencil, pens, street signs, tapes, tape recorders, telephone, telegram, trademarks, traffic signals, wet clothes, wheels.

PLACES

The banks, bookshelves, book stores, colleges, cooperative units, the Consulate offices, dining halls, drawing-rooms, the Educational institutions, schools, educational seminars, conferences and academies, empty grounds, furniture, furniture showrooms, gardens, green meadows, high ways, libraries, northern direction, offices of the astrologers, the accountants and the auditors, parks, play grounds, post offices, printing houses of newspapers, magazines and books, printing press, stadium, stock exchanges, study-halls, tax collecting places, telephone exchanges, telephone booths, the Universities, vacant lands, windows.

PROFESSION

Accountants, academicians, actors, advisors, agents, ambassadors, anchors of radio and television and other media programmers, announcer, apprentices, artists, astrologers, auditors, authors, bankers, book sellers, broadcaster, brokers, businessmen, cab service, circus artists, clerks, clowns, comedians, commentators, commission agents, communicators, consultants, correspondents, counselors, courier agents, cryptologist, dancers, dance master, document writers, dealers of intoxicating substances, dealers of two and four wheelers, diplomats, drivers, editors, educationists, gem testing, guides, insurance agents, investigators, jesters, journalists, jugglers, lawyers, lecturers, mathematicians, mediators, middle men, mimicry artists, musicians, music teacher, news editors, news readers, orators, orchestra conductors, paddy merchants, painters, photographers, planners, postmen, preachers, printers, programmers, propagandists, publishers, public relations officer, real estate dealers, receptionists, record clerk, registrar, reporters, representatives, research scholars, retail traders, salesmen, sculptors, secretaries, singers, stamp vendors, stationery shop owners, statistician, taxi service, teachers, telephone operators, tourist operators, transport department, travel, tutors, writers.

RELATIONS

The adopted child is the Kaaraka of the Mercury. The maternal uncle, the aunt, the friends, the younger sister, the lover, the assistants, the helpers, the young calves of animals and the younger group of persons are represented by the Mercury.

RELIGION

Shree Vishnu in all His forms and avatars is denoted by the Mercury. The Saptha Kannimargal, the Gandharvas are represented by the Mercury. The Vaishnavism cult is the Kaaraka of the Mercury.

THE JUPITER

GENERAL

The Jupiter or the Guru is the largest of all the planets. Its diameter is 1.43 lakh kilometers, more than 11 times that of the Earth. It is at an average distance of about 77.85 crore kilometers from the Sun. The planet completes one orbital round in about 4,333 Earth days or almost 12 Earth years. Ancient Romans named it after their god Jupiter. The Jupiter rules over the stars the Punarvasu, the Vishaka and the Poorva Bhadrapada and the signs the Dhanus and the Meena. It gets exalted in Cancer and faces its fall in Capricorn. The dasa period extends for 16 years. To cover on Nakshtra pada the Jupiter takes 40 days and 12 hours and in a sign Guru stays for a period of about one year. The Jupiter rotates faster in its axis compared to any other planet. The duration of one day in the Jupiter is of around 10 Earth hours.

The most auspicious of the entire planets, the Jupiter indicates all the good things and the prosperity. When the Jupiter conjoins or aspects any planet, that planet would also become benefic. Accommodative nature, acumen, advisor, affable qualities, affectionate behaviour, affluent, kindness, awards, barristers, benevolence, bishops, Brahmins, broad mindedness, buoyant, candid, celebrities, charitable, chastity, children, Chief Ministers, clergy, codes, compassion, Constitution, contentment, Countries, decency, decorum, determination, devotion, dignity, discipline, divine, dutiful, enacted laws, endowments, Epics, expansion, fame, foreign aid, fortune, generous, genuine, gold, golden hue, good health, good-humour, governess, Governors, grants, happiness, heritage, highly respectable, holy books, holy matters, holy men, holy scriptures, honesty, honour, hospitality, impartial, impeccable conduct, improvement, integrity, jovial, jubilations, judicial, judicious, judgment, judges, large animals, law, law abiding quality, learning, literature, loans, male progeny, mass production, mediation, mild, ministers, modest, money in large sum, optimism, opulence, passports, patience, peacefulness, philanthropy, philosophy, physicians, pilgrimage, places of worship, prayers, probity, professional people, progeny, popularity, prizes, purity, reasoning ability, refund, reputation, resourceful, respect for elders, rules and regulations, Sanskrit and Telugu languages, scholarly, self-confidence, self-control, sense of judgment, sincerity, social conscious, spiritual awareness, spiritual pursuits, stationery shop, steadfastness, sterling character, straight forwardness, success, summons, theology, titles, treasure, treasury, trustworthiness, truth, umpires, validity, value, valuables, virtuous, wages, wealth, wisdom, yellow colour.

BODY PARTS AND DISEASES

The brain, cholesterol, circulation of the blood, ears, fats, flesh, functions of the heart, functions of all the muscular parts of the body, gall bladder, general wellbeing, liver, lungs, nose, pancreas, spleen, stomach, thighs, veins, wavy hair are indicated by the Jupiter.

The abscess, asthma, atherosclerosis, blood clots, boils, cancer, carbuncle, diabetes, dropsy, dyspepsia, ear ailments, fainting, flatulence, gall bladder disease, indigestion, jaundice, liver disorders, obesity, respiratory disorders, swelling of body parts, vertigo are the diseases connected with the Jupiter.

OBJECTS

All auspicious things, banyan tree, butter, cash box, certificates, chariots, coconut tree, cotton, cows, cumin seeds, the Dividends, elephants, fenugreek seeds, fruits, fruit bearing tress, ghee, gold, holy books, honey, horses, jasmine, jack fruit, license, medallions, passport, peepul tree, platinum, rain, rubber, ships, silk clothes, swan, sweet confectionery, tin, traditional food varieties, turmeric are the Kaaraka of the Jupiter.

PLACES

The academies, assemblies, administrative centers, all religious places, banks, bridges, coronation halls, hamlets of Brahmins, hospitals, hostels, meditation and yoga centers, mines, money minting places, the religious mutts, north-eastern direction, the Parliament, the palaces, the places where the children enjoy playing, the places where money is kept, the places where gold is stored in huge quantities, places where auspicious things are kept, puja halls, the Reserve bank, the stock exchanges, the Supreme Court and the High Courts and the treasuries are represented by the Jupiter. The educational institutions are represented by the Jupiter.

PROFESSION

All types of work dealing with money, the astrologers, the brokers, the bullion trade, customs and excise department, the doctors, financers, jobs dealing with Sastras, the Judges, the lawyers, the Mutt heads, the preachers, prestigious jobs, the Prohits, the religious heads, the religious and spiritual rituals and duties, share trading, supervisors, teachers, temple administrators, temple priests, trust members and heads. The lecturers are denoted by the Mercury and the Professors who are higher in the hierarchy and the heads of the departments are denoted by the Jupiter.

RELATIONS

Indicates grand and great grandfathers and the children, sons, elder brother, father's elder brothers,

RELIGION

The deities where strict rules and regulations are followed as per the dictates of the scriptures for worshipping, the deities for whom the Pujas where conducted by the Brahmins, the Kula deiva, the Dhakshinamurty.

THE VENUS

GENERAL

The Venus or the Sukra is the second of the innermost planets. This is at a distance of about 67 million miles away from the Sun and has a periodicity of 244 days. The Venus always remains within 48 degrees from the Sun. In astronomy the Venus and the Earth are known as "twins" because of their similar size. The diameter of the Venus is about 12,100 kilometers, approximately 560 kilometers smaller than that of the Earth. The Venus got its name from the Roman goddess of beauty, gardens, love and sexuality. In Indian mythology the Venus is related to the goddess Shree Lakshmi who is known for her divine beauty and granting of immense wealth. The Venus takes about 225 Earth days to go around the Sun once. One year in the Venus is about seven and half months long. While the orbits of most of the planets are elliptical, the path of the Venus is almost a circle. The Venus revolves around the Sun in the same way as the Earth, but while rotating itself on its axis, it rotates in the opposite direction. The Sukra is the lord of the stars Bharani, Poorva phalguni, Poorvashada and the signs Rishaba and Thula. The Sukra is exalted in Meena and gets debilitated in Kanya. The dasa period of the Sukra is 20 years. The Venus takes about 3 days and 8 hours to cover one Nakshtra pada and 30 days to cover a sign. The Venus goes into retrograde once in 18 months for a period of 45 days. The Venus is a watery and feminine planet. The Sukra is supposed to possess the lifesaving power since he has mastered the Amrita Sanjeeveni Mantra which could bring back the dead to life.

The Venus is the planet of beauty. Anything and everything beautiful belongs to the Venus. The sparkling eyes, the delightful face, the plumpy cheeks, the glistening teeth, the curly hair, the tender fingers, the sweet voice are denoted by the Sukra. Artistic articles, aesthetic objects, fashionable items, stylish stuff, sophisticated possessions, luxurious household goods, elegant stuffs, premium vehicles and novel belongings are denoted by the Venus. The nature of the Venus is both artistic and attractive. Also, the Venus denotes both comforts and the luxury. The washing machine, the CCTV, the decorative lights and the high tech television sets are some more of the kaaraka of the Venus.

The liquor of superior quality is denoted by the Venus. The tea is also the kaaraka of the Venus. Likewise, the sweet candy, the fruit juices, the delicious eatables and the bakery munchies are represented by the planet Venus. The diseases related to the kidney, the diabetes, hormonal disturbances and the sexually transmitted diseases are marked by the Venus. Well placed Venus bestow one with the talents in the art and poetry and focus on love and romance.

The palatial houses, the five star hotels, the huge shopping malls, the super markets, the departmental stores, the cinema theatres, the banks, the marriage halls and the auditoriums are the kaarakathuvas of the Venus. The flowers and the orchards are the kaaraka of the Venus.

The Venus denotes the feminine gender. It signifies the accommodative tendency, adornment, affability, allurement, amorous activities or behavior or speech, arts, artistic talents, artistic interests, attraction, attachment, beauticians, beauty, bed room, bedroom pleasures, bright, brilliance, celebrations, charm, coitus, comforts, confectionery, concerts, conjugal life, coordination, creativity, culture, decorations, delicacy, delicious, delightful, diamond, diplomacy, donation, drama, dresses, elegance, embroidery, engagement, enjoyment, entertainments, eyes, festivals, flattery, freshness, friendship, fun, gambling houses, gentle, girls, glamour, grace. hair styles, handsomeness, honeymoon, illicit relations, infatuation, kindness, liquor, liquor bars, love, lust, luxury, marriage, marital happiness, materialistic pleasure, modesty, music, neat and tidy, ornaments, ostentation, passion, peacock, pearls, playful, pleasant, pleasure, poetry, polite, pomp and splendour, Rajo guna, recreations, refinement, romance, Sanskrit and Telugu languages, seduction, seducing eyes, semen, sensual pleasures, sexual activity, sexual desire, sexual drive, sexual pleasure, silk, smoothness, softness, Spring season, style, sweet dishes, sweetness, treasure, vanity, vehicles, virility, vitality, wealth, weaving, wine and youthfulness

BODY PARTS AND DISEASES

All hormonal secretions in the body, cheeks, chin, curly hair, face, kidney, ovaries, private parts, reproductive system, urinary system, sparkling eyes are denoted by the Venus.

Anemia, carbuncle, diabetes, diseases of the women, eye ailments, impotency, perversions, renal stones, sexual dysfunction, sexually transmitted diseases, thyroid dysfunctions, urinary disorders are some of the diseases associated with the Venus.

OBJECTS

Blue colour, bouquet, boutique shops, candy, cakes, cars, civet, comfort kits, cosmetics, cows, curd, decorative pieces, delicious food varieties, diamond, dress materials, dressing sense, embroidery designs, exquisite dresses, fancy articles, filigree work, fish, flowers, food grains, fragrant substances, fruits, fruit juices, ghee, glass utensils, honey, hyacinth bean, ivory, jasmine flower, jewelry, ladies utilities, liquor, luscious drinking items, luxurious products, makeup kits, mica, musical instruments, musk, paints, perfumes, photographs, pink colour, platinum, pleasant odours, readymade garments, sandalwood, sewing machines, silk, silver, sophisticated articles, strange objects, sugar, sugar cane, sweet stalls, toys, turquoise colour, umbrellas, white lotus flower, wigs are few of the objects connected with the Venus. Anything which is attractive, beautiful, comfortable, luxurious and sophisticated is the Kaaraka for the Venus. The Venus indicates the pleasures and recreations.

PLACES

Amusement centers, beauty parlour, bed chamber, brothel houses, cattle sheds, dance auditoriums, dining halls, drama theaters, entertainment centers, gift shops, harems, hotels, fashion malls, ladies' quarters, makeup rooms, marriage halls, massage parlours, palaces, parks, posh buildings, pubs, readymade shops, recreational houses, salons, south-eastern direction, studio, sweet stalls, textile outlets, theatre halls.

PROFESSION

The jobs which deal with the manufacturing and selling of all the objects used by the womenfolk like cosmetics, decorative articles, fashion materials, flowers, jewels, luxurious objects, make up kits, perfumes and saris are denoted by the Venus. The actors, the amusement artists, artistic forms, bakery, beauticians, brothel owners, cameramen, cattle rearing, costume designers, dance masters, dancers, designers, entertainers, the trade which deals with the gold, silver, diamond and precious gems, financiers, instrument players, jobs connected with the air travel, liquor shops, lodging houses, musicians, orchestra players, painters, personal secretaries, photographers, poets, prostitutes, receptionists, sale of articles like bed materials, cots, musical instruments, pet animals, silk saris, silverwares, intoxicating substances and vehicles, singers, tailors and textile shops are the notable professions connected with the Venus.

RELATIONS

Aunt, elder sister, mother's elder sisters, step mother, wife.

RELIGION

The Female deities which appear well decorated and richly costumed and ornamented are represented by the Venus. When in the conjunction with the Mercury, it denotes the female deities of the Vaishnavism and with the conjunction of the Sun and the Saturn indicates the Saivite female deities. The one eyed Asura Guru, the Sukracharya is signified by the planet Venus.

THE SATURN

GENERAL

The Saturn or the Sani is the farthest of all the planets from the Sun. The distance between them is about 143 crore kilometers. It is the slowest among the planets and the second largest. The Saturn takes about 30 years to complete one revolution around the zodiac. The Saturn is named after the Roman god of agriculture and he was the father of the Jupiter. In Indian mythology the Saturn is said to be the son of the Sun. The Saturn rules the houses Makara and Kumbha and the stars the Pushya, the Anuradha and the Uthra Bhadrapada. It gets exalted in the Thula and becomes debilitated in the Mesha. The Saturn is a cool, dry and an airy planet. The Saturn is the kaaraka for Democracy. The common population and the people in the lower echelons of the society are denoted by the Saturn only. The dasa period of the Saturn is 19 years. The Saturn takes generally 30 months to transit a Rasi. The Saturn rotates on its axis very fast and it is the second next to the Jupiter's rotation. One day is around 10.25 hours long in the Saturn. Astronomically the Saturn takes nearly 29.46 years to complete one revolution around the Sun. The mass of the Saturn is about 95 times that of the Earth.

The special feature of the Saturn is its slow movement. So the native will realise the Kaaraka of the Saturn delayed only. Suppose, the Saturn is placed in the 4th house. The chances of getting an own house will take a long time. If it is in the 5th, the progeny will be delayed. But, it is with good only. While the Saturn delivers its fortunes slow, they last longer. The house or the property bought in the dasa or the bhukthi of the Saturn, gets retained with the family for generations. Remember, the Saturday is called as Sthira vaar (fixed or permanent).

The main kaaraka of the Saturn is the profession. So those with the influence of the Saturn will be hard workers. In whatever job they are, they will have an inner urge to start a business of their own. They will like to do night time jobs because the Saturn represents the dark. Especially, the Makara natives are fond of working as this happens to be the 10th house of the Kaala Purusha.

The Saturn is basically simple and the workers which are denoted by the Saturn reflect the same quality. When you approach a rickshaw wallah or a coolie or such people in the lowest line of the work force, and ask them how much you should pay for doing a certain job, they will not tell you the rate. In turn, they will ask us how much you will give. This is the nature of the Saturn. And next thing they will say is you pay me after seeing my work. This is another attribute of the Saturn. They are proud of their work.

The honesty, simplicity, cowardice, inferiority complex, distrustful nature, loneliness, miserliness, elderly look, poverty, clumsy and unclean appearance, laziness, fearsome mentality and dejected mind are some of the characteristic features of the Saturn. The persons who are working as the servants and in the lower hierarchy in any orgainsation are represented by the Saturn. The Saturn denotes the physically challenged people.

Archeology, adulteration, adversity, anonymous persons, anonymous activities, anxiety, austere tendency, avaricious nature, barriers, barren, beggars, blue sapphire, blue colour, boundaries, bridges, calamity, caution, cheating, cold climate, concealment, conservative, constrictions, contemplative, cowardice, crooked nature, cruel deeds, dark, death, debts, decay, deceit, defeat, defensive, dejection, delay, dependence, depression, deserts, despondent, detachment, differences, difficulties, dirt, dirty places, disappointments, disease, dishonour, dislike, distress, downfall, downtrodden, drought, dry, dull, elders, elderly people, empty rhetoric, endurance, eunuch, fall, fatalities, footwear, foul smell, freeze, frugal, futile talk, garbage, gloom, granite, greed, grief, handicapped, handicraft, hard labour, hardship, heart ailments, hell, hesitation, ice, ill feelings, imprisonment, inferior, inferiority complex, incompatibility, inflexible, justice, judgment, judicious, jury, the Karma, lame, lazy, leader of the oppressed and the suppressed, lethargy, lifespan, loneliness, meditation, melancholy, misery, miserliness, misfortune, mourning, obedient, objections, obsolescence, obstacles, obstinacy, old, old age, omissions, oppressions, pain, patience, persistent, pottery, poverty, premature aging, profession, prudence, punishments, restrictions, scandals, secretive, selfish, sense of touch, servants, shabbiness, shameless, sin, slaves, slow, sluggish, sorrow, stagnation, starvation, stealing inclination, stones, strikes, stubbornness, subordinates, subservience, Thamo guna, traffic, troubles, ugliness, uneven body parts, unhappiness, vengeance, waste, weakness, weight, western direction, wickedness, wind, winter season, workaholic.

BODY PARTS AND DISEASES

Coarse hair, knees, knee caps, legs, skeleton, all the visible external nerves, teeth, feet are some of the parts indicated by the Saturn.

Arthritis, chronic ailments, constipation, defective limbs, diseases affecting the lower parts of the body such us foot, dull pains, dysfunction of organs, fatigue, Filaria, heart ailments, incurable diseases, insanity, leprosy, mutilated body parts, paralysis, rheumatism, tumours. The onset of the diseases denoted by the Saturn takes a lengthy time. They manifest with dull aching pain and are chronic in nature. The recovery also takes a long time.

OBJECTS

Ancient things, belts, black colour, black gram, blue coloured articles, blue sapphire, bricks, buffaloes, cement, clocks, coal, contaminated and stale food, dirty and indecent objects, dogs, donkeys, gingely oil, hair, ice, iron and steel, jute, kerosene, lead, leather, locks, minerals, memorials, metals, oil varieties, old articles, petrol, sand, sesame, shoes, toilets, useless articles, useless vegetation, weighing scale, wool.

PLACES

Dark places, dark holes, dirty areas, barber's shop, dilapidated houses, grave yards, junctions, leather tanneries, mines, mortuary rooms, old buildings, pits, places with foul and pungent odour, secret hideouts, slums, toilets, unclean places are denoted by the Saturn.

PROFESSION

Agriculturists, barbers, beggar, broker, butcher, cattle rearing, cleaners, cobblers, coffin makers, cooks, dealers of second hand or old products, hardware shop keepers, hermits, iron merchants, jailor, jobs in the lower hierarchy in any system like the peons, the attenders, the servers etc., leaders of the downtrodden and underprivileged masses, low paid, the low esteemed and the mean jobs, manual laboures, oil mongers, people working with death like in the grave yard or in the mortuary, persons in the crematorium, pig rearing, potter, researchers, scavenger, servers, selling of black coloured objects like the coal, slaves, tannery workers, waste products disposal, watchmen, wood cutters, works involving severe body labour are some of the professions indicated by the Saturn.

Note:

The broker job has been signified by the planets the Jupiter, the Mercury and the Saturn. But there is a difference in their job function. The Mercury is the real broker in all the senses of the term. The Jupiter is not a broker by profession and his services may not involve monetary benefits but they may be more of referral and friendly natured. But the Saturn as a broker is a cheat.

RELATIONS

Elder brother, elderly people, father's younger brother, servants.

RELIGION

The Saturn is the embodiment of the Karma principle of the Indian tradition. Mainly all the deities worshipped as the protectors like the Iyyanar, the Karuppu etc., are indicated by the Saturn. The ancient temples and the gods there are denoted by the Saturn. The Saturn denotes old, dilapidated, abandoned and neglected places of worship.

THE RAHU

GENERAL

In the Jamakkol prasanam the Rahu and the Ketu are combined together and treated as a single entity as the Snake. Here we don't differentiate it as the Rahu or the Ketu. But for the understanding of the Kaarakathuvas, their significators are dealt separately in detail here. This is for the general awareness of the Kaarakathuva features.

The Rahu and the Ketu are the points of intersection of the orbits of the Moon and the Sun around the Earth. They are called as Ascending node, the Rahu and the Descending node, the Ketu. The Rahu is called as the Dragon's head or Caput. These sensitive points the Rahu and the Ketu are given the status of planets in the Indian astrology and are called as shadowy planets. The Rahu rules over the stars the Ardra, the Swathi and the Sadhabishak. The Dasa period of the Rahu is 18 years.

The Rahu takes roughly 18 months to transit a sign and two months to transit a Nakshtra pada. The Rahu and the Ketu do not have ownership of signs. But at the same time, there are various opinions available about their Moola Trikona, exalted or debilitated houses. They each stay for 18 months in a sign and they are always 180 degrees apart to each other. They always move in anti-clockwise direction or in ever retrograde motion.

The Rahu and the Ketu are called as the shadowy planets. So they refer to shadows or images or copies. The professions which are connected with shadows or the images are hence represented by the Rahu. For example, the photography, the photostat work, the X ray, the scan, the MRI, the cinema, the television, the printing work etc., are all represented by the Rahu.

The Rahu refers to the past generation. That is our fore fathers. At the same time the Rahu is the kaaraka for the modern things like the electronic gadgets. The persons with the influence of the Rahu will not get sleep easily. They will roll in their bed for a long time. Particularly the persons with the Rahu in the 12th house will get very disturbed and a poor sleep only during the night. The 12th house signifies the sayana suga.

The abduction, abductors, abortions, accidents or diseases which involve permanent loss or dysfunction of body organs, addictions, adulteration, adultery, alcohol, amputations, anesthetics, ants, asbestos, assassination, blackmail, bore wells, chemicals, clouds, cloudiness, collection of interest to the loans given, confinement, confusions, conspiracy, contaminated food, conversion, counterfeit, crime, criminals, criminal activities, crisis, critical situations, cyclones, death sentence, deceitful nature, deformity, deserts, deserted regions, detention, disguise, disinfectants, doping substances, drown, drugs, drug less healing techniques, dubious personality, duplicates, eccentricity, electrical and electronic objects and their servicing, elephants, evil spirits, evil thoughts, evil and treacherous plots and activities, exile, extra sensory perceptions, fake, fanatics, fears, fertilizers, fraud, falsehood, foreigners, foreign languages, foreign places, forests, gambling, gigantic, ghosts, guerilla warfare, hanging, harsh words, hermaphrodite behaviour, high mountains, homosexuality, huge, hypnotism, illegal activities, illicit affairs, illogical speech, illusion, immoral sexual behaviour, imprisonment, inaccessible places, incest, insecticides, incest, intelligence, intoxicating substances, intuition, iron and steel, jackal, kidnapping, liar, lies, loitering, loosing ones' ancestry, looting, mass deaths. mica, mining, misuse of power and authority, murder, notoriety, occult practices, owls, pawn broking, payment of interest to the loans incurred, paralysis, petrol extraction, phobia, physical contact with elderly women or widows, pilgrimage, piracy, plastic objects, pleasurable acts, poison, poisoning, poisonous bites, poisonous insects, political murders, poverty, prisons, prostitutes, prostitution, reptiles, researchers, rivers, robbery, rumours, sadism, sandal wood, scarcity, scandals, seduction, self-boasting, sense of hearing, sexually transmitted diseases, sexual perversions, shadows, smugglers, snakes, snake bites, snake charmers, smoke, smoking, south west direction, spider, spurious things, suicide, suicidal attempts, torture, unconventional, unorthodoxy, venomous activities and speech, worldly pleasures, yogic practices are some of the notable kaarakathuvas of the Rahu.

BODY PARTS AND DISEASES

The Lips, nails, mouth, skin, testicles are few of the parts described by the Rahu. The allergic reactions, cancer, carbuncle, contagious diseases, debility, those diseases that are difficult to diagnose, diseases of unknown origin, diseases connected with the pollution of air or water, diseases which result in unbearable pain and suffering, eclampsia, eczema, endemic and epidemic diseases like plague, the AIDS and the cholera, epilepsy, Filaria, food poisoning, hiccups, leprosy, leukoderma, malaria, mental disorders, polio, psoriasis, respiratory disorders, scabies, skin diseases, small pox, varicose veins, worm infestations are denoted by the Rahu.

OBJECTS

All those are glittering and shiny, alcoholic beverages, animal skins, bamboo, bed bugs, big checked or broad stripped dresses, black gram, blue colour, bright and flashy garments, bushes, cement, creepers, deep waters, detergents, dogs, dry skin, durva grass, electric lights, elephant tusk, hessonite, hides and skins, holes, jackal, mosquitoes, mustard, mustard oil, narcotic substances, oversized dresses, owls, pits, plastic and rubber articles, poisonous substances, sky, snails, spider, string, vinegar, umbrella.

PLACES

Ant hills, bushes, casinos, cavities, the Highways, mosques, pits, railway tracks, snake's habitats, stadium and the stock markets.

PROFESSION

All the jobs related to foreign assignments, air travel, astrology, black magic, cinema, detectives, electrical and electronic works, envoys, fluency in foreign languages, gambling, glass and porcelain business, honey bee rearing, hunting, illegal activities, imports and exports, media jobs, messengers, money lenders, new inventions, pawn brokers, pirates, printing, professions done in the dark like cinema, photography, Photostat, prostitution, sale of poisonous substances, television and x ray, research, sericulture, snake charmers, snake farms, spies, stealing, television, radio and watch service, travelling jobs are few of the jobs related to the Rahu.

RELATIONS

In the Male sign and in the male Navamsa the Rahu indicates the paternal grandfather and in the Female sign and in the female Navamsa it indicates the maternal grandfather. When it is the male sign and the female Navamsa or vice versa it indicates both the grand fathers. The widows, separated wives, widowers, separated husbands, adopted children are represented by the Rahu.

RELIGION

All the gods having nonhuman face like Shree Narasimha, Shree Hanuman, Shree Hayagriva, Shree Nandi, Shree Adhisesha etc., and the female deity the Durga, the religion of Islam and the Muslim community, Tantric system of worship are the Kaaraka of the Rahu.

THE KETU

GENERAL

In Western astrology the Ketu is called as the Dragon's tail or the Cauda. The Ketu is said to be the eldest among the planets. The God Vinayagar, who is said to the foremost among the Gods, is associated with the Ketu. One of the stars of the Ketu is the Moola, which means the root or the origin. All those significators assigned to the Rahu are applicable to the Ketu also. The Ketu rules over the stars of the Ashwini, the Magha and the Moola. The Dasa period is 7 years.

The Ketu is a mystic and a mysterious planet also. The features of the Ketu are not comprehensible easily. When the Ketu is placed in its own stars of the Ashwini, the Magha and the Moola, it will help the native to scale to greater heights in their life. The Ketu on one side has the spirulasitic tendencies. They may even be ready to depart from the family life and embrace the ascetic path. They are always depressed and deserted. On the other side, the Ketu possess the tricky criminal mind and propensities. They are schemers and they are deceitful. Their clandestine nature in a way makes them fit for the jobs like investigation, spying or vigilance. At the same time whatever the Ketu does, even if it is surreptitious, it will be legal and will be supported with proper evidence. Whereas the activities of the Rahu are always clandestine and unlawful.

The well placed Ketu gives the talents in the law, the medicine, the astrology and they are respectable teachers also. When the lagna is in the star of the Ketu or when the Ketu is in the lagna, the native or someone in their families will be in any of the above mentioned professions.

The hair, the tuft, and the beard are represented by the Ketu while the mustache is the kaaraka of the Mars. The things that one wears on their heads like the caps, the crown or the turbans are represented by the Ketu,

The Ketu represents the nets. Any net from the simple fishing net, spiders web, wire mesh, ropes, loops, fences, window nets, mesh lattices, mosquito nets, complex and complicated wire or net connections, electrical coils, electronic networks, traps, etc., to the Internet is signified by the Ketu. Even the web of love is denoted by the Ketu only. The spinning, the netting, rewinding, plaiting of the hair, the knitting works, making flowers as a garland, stitching, weaving etc., are some of the jobs connected to the Ketu.

Ascetic robes, activities connected with underground research and exploration, alchemy, all types of viral, bacterial or fungal infections, astrology, barley, bats, beard, blackmail, blind streets, camels, castor oil, celibacy, cemeteries, chemicals, clapping, cloth weaving, clothing or industry associated with animal fur and leather, coconuts, cockroaches, complications, concept of Karma, conspiracy, coughing, cowardly nature, criminals, dates, death, deserts, desert plantation, destitute, destruction, detachment, determination, difficulties, dip in holy waters, division, divorce, dogs, dog bites, drinking habit, dry places, eagles, ear rings, endurance, evil spirits, exorcism, flags, flag masts, flies, frustration, fungus, intestinal worms, glow worms, hidden treasure, homeless, horned animals and also their attacks, horse gram, hospitals, hunger, hypnotism, hypocrisy, impotency, infectious diseases, injections, inhospitable environments, legal matters, lice, life after death, male goat, medicinal substances, meditation, meteors, microscopic things, Moksha, mosquito, mushrooms, multi coloured clothes, mystery objects, narrow things, nose rings, north western direction, obstinacy, occult sciences, penance, philosophical, physical exercises, piercing, pilgrims, pilgrimage, pottery, poverty, prayers, prisons, psychic behaviour, rabies, refugees, religious, renunciation, sesame oil, sense of smell, separations, separatists, sharp things like needles or mustache or beard, silence, small checked or narrow thin striped garments, smoke, smoking, spiritual enlightenment, spirituality, starvation, sterile, strange objects, telepathy, tolerance, tribal lands, tribal people, uncultivable lands, uninhabited lands, wanderers, weavers, wicked mentality, winding job, worms.

BODY PARTS AND DISEASES

Anus, excretory organs, hair in the head and the body parts, the lips, the nervous system which is interring, the pimples are some of the body parts denoted by the Ketu.

Allergy, contagious diseases, eye diseases, diseases connected with the excretory organs like piles and fistula, fever, infections, leprosy, leukoderma, mental disorder, migraine, pain, scabies, scars, skin diseases, small pox, spasms, sprains, stomach ailments, urinary disorders, viral diseases, wounds are the common diseases associated with the Ketu.

OBJECTS

Aerial roots, ash, cats eye stone, chains, comets, dry grass, eagles, electrical cables, elephant's trunk, fishing nets, horse gram, injections, minute objects, neck tie, needles, nets, pots, ragged cloth, roots, ropes, spider web, tail, thin wire like structures, threads, tight fitting dresses.

PLACES

Back door of the house, blacksmiths' workshops, burial grounds, cemetery, cervices, charity homes, clefts, Court halls, holy places, hospitals, huts, law chambers, meditation halls, monasteries, museums, mutts, narrow lanes, places where hanging is executed, prisons, puja halls, staircase, tailoring shops, weaving centers.

PROFESSION

Archeologists, antique dealers, arbitrator, black magic, coil winding, detectives, doctors, electrical wiring, fishing, forensic experts, healers, hired killers, historians, lawyers, preachers, sellers of cement, coffee seeds, herbs, medicines, rubber objects, tea and tobacco, spies, spiritual and religious activities, surgeons, tailoring, typist, weaving. And all those professions that are described for the Rahu also suit the Ketu.

RELATIONS

In odd rasi and Navamsa the Ketu indicates the paternal grandmother and in even rasi and Navamsa indicates the maternal grandmother. In mixed placements indicates both the grand mothers. Very young children, very old people.

RELIGION

All gods having non-human faces and especially those having a tail like the Hanuman, the Sarabheswara, asceticism, the Christian religion, detachment, fasting and similar such rituals done for religious purposes, Lord Vinayagar, mediation, Moksha, monks, pilgrimage, renunciation, sacrificial offerings, sacrificial killings, saints, salvation, silent prayers are denoted by the Ketu.

2. Rasi Kaarakathuvam

The important kaarakathuvas of the twelve rasis are given here. What is the need for them? They are needed to identify and locate the places, objects, shapes, features etc., which are related to the query of the clients.

Mesha

The Mesha or the Aries extends from 0 to 30 degrees in the zodiac. This sign is represented by the symbol Ram. The sign represents the green pastures where the cattle are reared. The Mesha signifies the

Dharma house. The Mars is a Movable sign. These natives will be very active and seen moving here and there. These swift movements are denoted by the Mesha rasi. This house represents the Head of the Kaala Purusha. The Mars is the ruler and hence they might suffer from head ache or any such head related diseases like migraine, baldness, or health or other disorders. This sign represents the street beginning as it is the first sign of the zodiac. That means the person will have his house or shop (if it is the 10th house) at the very beginning of the street. Their houses will be low lying and so when it rains, their front side will be flooded or the water will be clogging there or the water will enter into their houses.

The Mars denotes the morning time between 6 to 8 a.m. The Mars is the ruler of this sign and also the Virschika which is the 8th from here. So thieves will hide themselves here or put their loot in this house. The Mars being their 8th lord, these natives are prone to accidents, surgeries or fire injuries. The 2nd house and the 7th house belongs to the Venus and so the wife (7) will be from a rich family (2). She will look after the finances of the house. The Mercury is the 3rd and the 6th lord. So they will have quarrel (6) with their neighbour regarding the compound wall. The Mars natives will have the Kataka as their 4th house. The Mars gets its debilitated state here. This house represents the heart and also movable and immovable properties. So it is likely that these natives get afflicted in these features. The Simha is the 5th house and almost to all the Mesha natives it bestows with children as it is the Puthra sthana of the Kaala Purusha. The 9th and the 12th lord Jupiter will give them spiritual inclinations in their later lives. The Saturn is the 10th as well as the 11th lord. So they will be profited well by their hard work in their profession. The precise nature of the Mesha are furious and daring.

Active, adamant, adventurous, aggressive, ambitious, animal sign, barren, battle fields, beginning of the street, boasting, bold, bricks, combativeness, cruel, dark red colour, decent, deserts, diurnal, diseases or injuries of the head and the brain, eastern direction, energy, enterprising, exhibitionism, extravagance, face, fickle minded, fiery, forests, frank, frequent travels, furious, green fields, guides, hasty, head, headstrong, high temperature zones, inaccessible places, independent, impatient, impulsive, jungles, kidney disorder, lands where treasures are hidden, leadership qualities, long ascension, masculine sign, meadows, middle stature, militancy, mines, morning time, mountains, movable, odd sign, pastures, pioneering, places where goats rear, places where stolen articles are kept, places where thieves hide, preachers, proud, prone to accidents and injuries, prushtodaya, quadruped sign, quarrelsome, red, reddish hue, resourceful, rough terrain, Ruby stone, sandy dunes, selfish, sleeplessness, slums, spontaneity, strong willed, stubborn, surgical operations, tenacious, thorny bushes, unorganized behaviour, villages, vehement nature, well ploughed land.

Rishaba

The Rishaba or the Taurus extends from 30 to 60 degrees in the zodiac. This sign is represented by the symbol bull. The Rishaba is an Artha sign. It is a feminine rasi. It has been classified as an Earthly Sign. The Venus is the lord of this house. So these people will like to enjoy the luxuries and the comforts of life. Their houses will be fitted or filled with the modern amenities like the air conditioners, washing machines, refrigerators, home theatres and the like. The banks or the ATMs, beauty parlours, ladies school or colleges or hostels will be nearer to their residences. The cattle will be reared or gazing near their places. The entertainment houses like the cinema theatres or galaxy halls, fun clubs, recreation centers, will be in their area. The Venus also owns the 6th house the Libra. So they will get affected by the debts or the diseases or the litigations. Most of them will be taking one or other tablet daily in their lifetime. The hormonal disturbances, particularly the thyroid and diabetes are seen frequently here.

The bull, the symbol of this sign is known for its chewing habits. Similarly, the natives of the Rishaba rasi will be bringing back their memories and thinking of them often. In earlier days the edible oils are extracted using a wood pressing machine called as Chekku in Tamil and this is pulled by the bulls. The bulls go round and round the machine a number of times in the process of oil extraction. Similarly, the natives of the sign Rishaba are not averse to the idea of doing things again and again and repeating the routine daily without a murmur. The bull used to draw the carts or plough the land carrying the burden on its back. Likewise, the Rishaba people are ready to shoulder or share others burdens willfully. The sign is described as the romantic and the relaxed.

The adamant behaviour, agriculture, agricultural lands, animal sign, appealing eyes, artistic interests, artistic talents, art works, banks, calm and patient nature and if provoked beyond a limit turns into wild and dangerous, cheerful, charming, center of the street, conservative, cowsheds, dependable, determined, earthly, enduring, even sign, face, feminine sign, fixed, fore head, friends, green meadows, lockers, long ascension sign, luxurious articles, love sign, materialistic, moist, neck, obstinate, persistent, pleasure seeking, plump, practical, prejudiced, proud, prushtodaya, secret chambers, secretive nature, self-boasting, selfish, strong at night, slow, stable, steady, sweet toothed nature, subjugation, taverns, treasury, white colour, windy character.

Mithuna

The Mithuna or the Gemini extends from 60 to 90 degrees in the zodiac. The Mithuna is illustrated by a couple. One of them holds a club and the other a veena. This sign represents the Kaama house. The Mithuna is a masculine rasi and a Upaya rasi. It is classified as an airy sign. People with the Mithuna will have their residences at the turning points of the streets. Their houses will have gardens. Or some parks or play grounds or the libraries or any educational institutions will be near their houses. This is the third house of the Kaala Purusha. Therefore, these natives are good communicators. They are generally good orators. They want someone listen to them and talking is the passion for them. They have artistic inclinations. Their 10th house of profession falls in the Pisces which is the house of the Jupiter. So teaching, astrology, law and banking related jobs attract them. Their career will bring them honour and status.

Since the 10th house is a Common sign, they may have two types of jobs, or they may work at two different places. In these situations of two jobs, one job they will do for monetary benefits and the other one they do it for job satisfaction or for service inclination. They usually shine well in their jobs. They grasp matters very easily and quickly. The 5th lord Venus is also the lord of their 12th house. This disrupts their getting an early progeny. The sign represents the arms, shoulders and the skin. The Mithuna rasi is noted for its communication and computing talents.

Academic seminars, airy, air travels, amusement centers, anxiety, arms, auditorium for dance, music and other artistic and cultural events, barren, biped sign, clever, commercial areas, common sign, communicative, communication of all types, copulating places, cruel, detective, dual nature, educational institutions, frequent travels (mostly shorter ones), gambling dens, grasping capacity, inconsistent, influenza, investigative nature, knowledgeable, lengthy limbs, light green colour, lungs, masculine sign, materialistic, mute, moving in villages, narrow lanes, neck, nervous, odd sign, orchards, parks, places where indoor games were played, play grounds, pleasing manners, pneumonia, quick witted, recreational activities, respiration, restless, retail sales, seershaodaya, strong at night, sexual experiences, shoulders, studious, study rooms, sweet voice, tall stature, timid, tuberculosis, unfinished works, urban setting, vivacious quality, voice.

Kataka

The Kataka or the Cancer extends from 90 to 120 degrees in the zodiac. The Kataka is symbolized by a crab. The Kataka belongs to the triplet of the Moksha houses. It is a feminine sign and a watery house. Being it the fourth bhava, the Kataka indicates fields and watery areas. They are interested in social service. It is a movable sign. The professions related to the milk and its products and also the import and export trade suits them. The ruler of this sign, the Moon denotes the food. So the jobs connected to the food items and food products is also good for them.

The Kataka also refers to the government buildings and quarters. Their 6th and the 9th lord is the Guru. So their father might be affected by some illness or litigation or debts. Their 3rd lord Mercury also holds the 12th house which brings them losses due to younger brethren. Similarly, the 11th lord Venus is also the Bhadaha adhipathi for the Kataka natives. So they might land up into problems due to the elder siblings or through the friends or through women. The Cancer sign refers to the mother. The mother is known for her care on her children, nourishment, affection and the way she protects her child/children. These qualities find place in the character of the Cancer natives. The Cancer sign is known for its emotion and nourishment.

Adaptable, administrative, affectionate, agricultural lands, attachment towards brothers, blood vessels going towards the heart, cancer disease, cautious, dairy farms, dexterous, diplomatic, discreet, dwarf, emotional, even sign, feminine sign, frugal, fruitful, honest, humid areas, hysterical, imaginative, industrious, inquisitive, intestine, irritable, movable, millipede, mute, nocturnal, non-vegetarian, over sensitive, perceptive, phlegm, politics, prone to accidents, prushtodaya, public service, rivers, river banks, river beds, sand dunes, sea shores, shrubs, stagnant, strong at night, sympathetic, talkative, tenacious memory power, washer men, washing areas, weak physique, watery, water pumps, watery places and areas nearby them, whitish red colour. The kaaraka relatives indicated by the planet(s) positioned in Kataka usually suffer.

Simha

The Simha or the Leo is represented by the symbol Lion and is ruled by the Sun. This sign extends from 120 to 150 degrees in the zodiac. This is one of the Dharma houses. This is a masculine and a fixed rasi. The sign is of Fiery nature. It denotes the heart and the stomach. The sign represents the hilly places, forests, forts, mounds, administrative buildings, casinos, deserts, government residential quarters, lodging houses, doctors' clinics, Jwellery shops, political and party headquarters government offices, government buildings, Lord Shiva temples, offices of the Presidents, the Prime Ministers and the Chief Ministers and public buildings, to name a few. The natives have high imagination and they fantasize everything. They are great dreamers. In which ever bhava the Sun is placed, the native will have high expectation and imagination about the kaaraka of that particular bhava. They are interested in the share market business. These people are independent and never like to be controlled or guided. They usually live or work in the upstairs. Their success in their marital life is average only. There are many reasons for that like their ego, independent nature, day dreams and expectations about marriage, the spouse and a delayed progeny. Moreover, their 7th lord, the Saturn also owns the 6th house (12th to the kalathra house). For Simha women, the Mars which represents the husbands, is also the bhadaha adhipathi of this sign. This sign can be described as autonomy and authority, mighty and magnanimous.

The active nature, administration, administrator, administrative capacity, administrative committee, administrative offices, adventurous, alertness, ambitious, analytical, animal sign, authority, avaricious, barren, boasting, bold, bones, bone marrow, brilliant, castles, caves, commanding, dense forests, deserts, determination, dignified, doctors, dry, earnestness, elevated places, entertainments, extravagance, fiery, firm, fixed, fleshy, forbearance, forgiveness, forts, furious persons, gambling, games, generous, gold, the Government, government buildings, government jobs, government offices, government in all its forms and purposes, grandeur nature, heart, heart ailments, high altitudes, hillock, hills, independent nature, ingenious, jungles, lavishness, leadership qualities, living in fantasy, lodging houses, magnanimous, majestic, mansions, markets, masculinity, mountains, muscular, noble, obstinate, odd sign, palaces, philosophical, politics, political career, politicians, political parties, power, power-crazy, rocky places, Royal qualities, self-respect, self-confidence, smartness, smoky white colour, speculation, spinal cord, spiritualism, sports, stadium, stock exchanges, stomach, tall, tough, trust worthiness, vertebrae, virility, weakness for flattery, well-built physique, wild animals are indicated by this sign.

Kanya

The Kanya or the Virgo extends from 150 to 180 degrees in the zodiac. The Virgo is symbolized by a virgin in a canoe carrying a fire pot in one hand and a sickle in the other hand. This sign represents Artha house. This is a feminine rasi and an earthly sign. This is a barren sign and their 5th lord the Saturn is also the owner of the 6th sign. So their progeny often gets delayed and the age difference between the first and the next child will be high. This sign represents both dry and wet agricultural lands. This is the sign of conglomeration. The academic scholars are represented here. In this sign they gather to learn. Likewise, this also indicates the libraries which are the collection centers of the books. Any farmstead is represented by this sign, be it cattle farm or the insect breeding centers. The retail shopping is one of the karakas of this sign. This sign is noted for its commercial talents and youthful looks.

Analytical, artistic skills, astrology, barren, biped sign, cities, clinics, cold, common sign, constipation, delayed childbirth, discriminative, dry, dual natured, earthly, educational institutions, even sign, feminine sign, good critic, good memory, good grasping poser, honesty, indigestion, industrial towns, libraries, lower portion of the spinal cord, magnanimous, navel, nocturnal, nursing homes, orchards, parks, pastoral lands, pharmacy, play houses, practical, prudent on financial matters, secret missions, self-conscious, seershaodaya, shy, societies, spiritualism, stomach, strong during the day, suspicious mind, systematic, talkative, towns, trustworthy, variegated colour, wet and dry lands, wholesale and large scale business establishments, youthful.

Thula

The Thula or the Libra extends from 180 to 210 degrees in the zodiac. The Thula is symbolized by a man holding a balance and sitting in the market. This sign belongs to the Kaama category of houses. This is a masculine sign and an airy sign too. This belongs to the movable sign. This sign indicates trading business. The native or his family must have done or doing some business or the other. Usually these natives have two names or their names will be two syllabled. Some people will have pseudonym or pet names. They judge a person correctly. This sign is the kalathra sthana of the Kaala Purusha. This sign therefore, denotes both the love and the lust. The Sun gets debilitated here. The Sun indicates the administration or the management. So if these natives are engaged in their own business, they should not look after the administration themselves. The Mercury is the owner of the 9th and the 12th house. So these natives will experience losses due to their father or they may lose their father early in life. The seventh house for them is the Mesha. The Mars is the owner of this house. So the life partner for the Thula natives will be adventurous, adamant, courageous, dominant, egoistic and they look after the administration of the domestic affairs. They have a very sharp grasping nature. The Venus is the ruler of the Rishaba also which is the 8th sign from the Thula. So the natives will possess intuitive nature. The natives will get benefits from the kaaraka of the

8th bhava like the Insurance, gains through the Will and unexpected money. The Thula rasi is noted for its judgement skills and jolly nature.

Aero planes, airy, authority in legal matters, bazaar, biped, black colour, business minded, business establishments, charming manners, chatterer, connoisseur of arts, courteous, court halls, dress materials, ornaments and other luxuries of life, early morning time, fair judgment, few children, fickle mind, frequent travels, graceful, handsome, idealistic, judgmental, kidney, kidney troubles, lecherous, market places, masculine, merchants, modest, movable, odd sign, prestige, pseudonym, river beds, roads, tall, unbiased, uterus, vindictive, well proportionate physique, youthful looks.

Virschika

The Virschika or the Scorpio extends from 210 to 240 degrees in the zodiac. This sign is represented by the insect Scorpio. This house belongs to the Moksha category. This is watery sign and a feminine sign. The Virschika is a fixed sign. This symbol of this sign is an insect Scorpio and most of the insects are having multiple foot. So when this sign indicates vehicles, it means the one with multiple wheels, buildings means multi storied, business establishments means departmental stores or shopping malls, organisation means that which possess many branches etc., This is how this kaaraka is used in prediction. This sign is known for its ability to keep their secrets within themselves. It is hard to crack their minds. Similarly, they will keep others confidential matters also undisclosed. The ability to withhold their secrets and the capacity to extract the secrets of the others makes them the ideal candidates for jobs like investigators, extractors and excavators. This sign denotes the excretory parts in a human body. Likewise, the dustbins, the gutters and the wastes are denoted by the sign.

It is said that the off springs of the scorpion are born after tearing open the mother's body and in that process the mother dies. So the quality of sacrificing for others is inbuilt in this sign. Being this the 8th house of the Kaala Purusha, they are interested in mystics, black magic and other such acts.

This sign indicates the dark and the hidden parts of the mind and the body. Being it a Keeta (insect) rasi, the insects thrive here. This sign denotes the perverted and immoral sexual behaviour. The age. convention, custom or social norms do not forbid them in their carnal hunts. The Mano kaaraka Moon is getting its debilitated state here. Moreover, the Kataka rasi is the bhadaha sthana for this sign. The lagna adhipathi of this sign gets debilitated at the Kataka.

Acids, acidic chambers, anus, arrack brewing places, arrack shops, bombs, burial grounds, cavities, cervices, cemetery, chemicals, chemical laboratories, coma stage, courageous, dams, deep pits, drains, empathetic, even sign, excretory organs, explosives, extravagance, feminine, firm, fixed, fruitful, genital organs, golden colour, gutters, hide-outs, hypocritical, imaginative, independent, intelligent, introvert, jealousy, Keeta (reptile) sign, kidney, knives, laboratory, lakes, liquor, long accession, marshy places, mysterious nature, nauseating and foul smell, narrow cavities, operation theatres, ovary, perseverance, petroleum products, pits, poisonous, poisonous insects, poisonous substances, pride, prostate glands, pungent odour, revengeful, sarcastic, secretive, self-reliant, self-respect, sexually transmitted disease, sewages, short stature, simpleton, slaughter houses, stagnancy, stagnant water, swords, tanneries, toilets, troublesome childhood, unclean, unyielding behaviour, urinary bladder, valleys, violent quality, viscous oils and liquids, watery sign, wells, wicked mind are some of the major kaarakathuvas of the Virschika rasi.

Dhanus

The Dhanus or the Sagittarius extends from 240 to 270 degrees in the zodiac. The Dhanus is represented by the figure whose upper half is in the form of a human being holding a bow and arrow in his hands and the rear half is represented by a horse with four legs. This sign belongs to the Dharma principle as this is the 9th sign of the Kaala Purusha. This is a masculine, common and a fiery sign. The symbol of this sign shows a bow and arrow and it is the only sign which carries a weapon. The archer requires a precise aim and a full concentration. These Dhanus natives are also endowed with the ability of hitting the bulls eye correctly. They know what they need and they also know how to get it.

It is said that the Kurushekthra war was fought in this sign. This sign is the symbol of the piercing arsenals and also sharp intelligence. The battle and the Bhagavad Gita were both born here. These natives like to teach and preach as this happens to be the 9th house of the Kaal Purusha. The Gita is again an example here. The sign represents the sports grounds, gym, ordinance factories, places where weapons are manufactured, places where the weapons are stored, martial arts, coaching centers of such activities like boxing, karate, wrestling, etc., Generally, the Dhanus natives are inclined to spirituality.

Achievement of the goals, archery, aspiration, barracks of animals like horses or elephants, battle grounds, boils, bravery, brownish colour, buttocks, charming, common sign, compassionate, cooperative societies, court halls, devotion, dry, dual sign, educational institutions, elephants, fiery sign, foreign affairs, friendly, Guru, handsomeness, higher echelon of knowledge, higher education, horses, hot, judicial, judgment, jungle, long travels, masculine sign, nervous disorders, newspapers, night time, odd sign, pawn broking places, philosophical matters, places of worship, plants, prushtodaya, religious, right decisions, servants, service mentality, spiritualistic education, spiritual people, tall, the thighs, teachers, temples, trees, warring mentality, weapons, well execution of plans, well-formed physique, wounds are represented by the Dhanus rasi.

Makara

The Makara or the Capricorn extends from 270 to 300 degrees of the zodiac. This sign belongs to the Artha principle. This sign is symbolized by a creature whose head is that of a stag and the rear part of the body that of a crocodile. This sign is classified as a watery sign but can be assumed to refer the combination of land and water, that is marshy surface. It's a feminine sign. The Makara is the 10th house of the Kaal Purusha. So, these natives are generally fond of working. They carve for recognition for their efforts. More than the monetary part, they need titles or posts or awards for their work. The rodents, the pigs, the crows, the washer men, washing areas, metals etc., are denoted by this sign. In any situation the Makara natives behave in the normal and in the most practical ways. This practicality has earned them the bad name that they are less empathetic and ruthless.

Their 4th lord Mars is also their 11th lord and hence it becomes the Bhadaha adhipathi. So they will have problems or dissatisfaction with their house, vehicles, properties etc., With all the 4th bhava kaaraka, they have a grievance. The Jupiter is their 3rd and the 12th lord. Due to this, their brothers (3) will be living in abroad (12) or they will incur losses (12) due to their brother (3). The Mercury is the 6th and the 9th lord. Therefore, the job (6) will come to them on its own. Similarly, the debts, diseases, the litigations will also seek them automatically.

The ancestral business, burial grounds, caves, cavities, dirty places, earthly sign, even sign, feminine sign, garbage, greedy, gutters, huts, inheriting father's profession, jungles, knee problems, marshy lands, movable sign, mortuary, mosques, pits, prisons, prushtodaya, rivers, river beds, sea shores, secret hideouts, selfish, self-boasting, the sewages, skilled work, skin diseases, strong at night, yellowish white colour are some of the significant karakas of the Makara rasi.

Kumbha

The Kumbha or the Aquarius extends from 300 to 330 degrees on the zodiac. The Kumbha is represented by a human carrying a water pitcher on his back. Whether the pitcher is empty or water-filled is a debating topic in astrology. Like, that these people will also be secretive in their activities. This sign belongs to the category of the Kaama houses. This is an airy sign. These people are characterized by their adamant nature, inquisitive mind and the dare devil approach. They have strong views and they will not get convinced and change even if it is proved that they are wrong.

This is the Labha house of the Kaal Purusha. The Dhana Kaaraka Jupiter is their 2nd and 11th lord. So their mind, words and activities always revolve round the gains which they might get in any pursuit. They handle finances well. This sign is a fixed sign. The symbol of this sign water pot will remain in the same place unless someone moves it. Similarly, these natives work, live and stay in a place for longer periods of time.

The adamant nature, administrative ability, airy sign, air service, anemic, artistic mind, asthmatic trouble, astronomy, biped sign, blood circulation, dark sign, diseases difficult to diagnose, drunkard, fixed sign, grayish white colour, hyper tension, inclination towards research, inflexible, lazy, legs, liquor shops, masculine sign, mid night, mysterious, patients, places where people assemble to draw drinking water like wells or taps, places where radio and television are kept in the house, potters, procrastination, researchers, respiratory disorders, secretive, short ascension, strong at day, ups and downs.

Meena

The Meena rasi or the sign of the Pisces extends from 330 to 360 degrees in the zodiac. This sign is represented by a pair of two fishes each facing in opposite directions and one of their head touching the tail of the other. The Meena rasi belongs to the Moksha house. This is a feminine sign. This sign represents the feet of the Kaala Purusha. This sign is the 12th sign of the zodiac. So it indicates long travels, particularly, abroad. The export and import business is also indicated here. They travel a lot. They don't like to shoulder responsibilities. They are slippery like their sign logo, the fish. Often, they are quite indecisive. Like the two fish which travel in opposite directions, they are also vacillating in extremes. The duality of their nature is not ruled out. This characteristic feature puts them in the verge of not trust worthy. Being the 12th sign of the zodiac this sign denotes the last stage of human life - the parting away from the worldly affairs and attachments. Their imaginative nature puts them in the fields of arts, music, painting, etc.,

The bathing Ghats, benevolent quality, common sign, deep wells, earth quakes, even sign, feminine sign, foot in the human body, holy places, holy rivers, hospitality, imaginative sign, indecisive, inflamed or injured or afflicted legs or fingers, innocent, knowledgeable, lazy, passionate, philosophic thought and tendencies, ponds, religious places, seas, strong both in day and night, short ascension, simple living, still waters, sympathetic nature, talkative, tanneries, ubhayodaya rasi, watery sign, white colour are the notable kaaraka of the Meena rasi.

The Kataka, the Simha, the Kanya, the Thula, the Virschika and the Dhanus are called as the Long ascension signs because they ascend in a longer time and the Makara, the Kumbha, the Meena, the Mesha, the Rishaba and the Mithuna are called as the Short ascension signs because they take shorter time to ascend. The duration of each rasis is around 2 hours only. But, some rasis take longer time to ascend this and some other rasis take shorter time.

3. Bhava Kaarakathuvams

First Bhava

This Bhava is called as the Lagna and it signifies all the general features and characteristics of the native. The features of this bhava are almost fixed and never change like the physical appearance, complexion. shape of the head etc.,

Ability, activity, administrative capacity, age, ambitions, ancestry, appearance, asceticism, attitudes, beauty, birth, body limbs, brain, character, childhood, culture, comforts and discomforts, courage, complexion, caste or community, character, characteristic marks, dignity, dreams, ego, environments at the time of birth, failures, fame, fortune, general disposition, grief, hair style, happiness, head, health, height, honesty, honour and dishonour, identity, immunity, infantile life, intelligence, knowledge, livelihood, longevity, magnanimity, mentality, native place, old age, perceptions, personality, physical constitution, physique, pride, prosperity, purpose of life, quality of life, recovery from illness, scholarly nature, self-respect, shape, stamina, standard of life, status, struggles in life, success, temperaments, tendencies, texture of the body, travel, vitality, wellbeing, wisdom.

Second Bhava

The addition of a member in the family may be it the spouse or the child, ambitions, bank balance, business, buying and selling, charity, chastity, cheeks, chin, clothes, copper, cosmetics, dependents, determination, eating habits, education, eloquence, eyes, eye brows, eye sight, face, family, finance, food, followers, friends, gait, gems, gold, grains, hospitality, humility, imagination, income, inheritance, jewels, lips, literary pursuits, luck, lustier of the face, manner and source of death, material assets, material prosperity, members of the family, miserliness, money, nails, neck, nose, observance of traffic rules, observation capacity, optimism, pearls, persons close by, pleasant speech, poetic outlook, popularity, power, proficiency in languages, profits and losses, purchase and sale of goods, quality of speech, rearing of pet animals, religious belief, resources, respect for culture and tradition, right eye, self-acquired wealth, self-earning capacity, silver, speech, speech organs, stocks and shares, share market, sweet voice, teeth, throat, tongue, vehicles, vision, wealth, worldly possessions, Maraka sthana.

Third Bhava

Ability, adaptability, arguments, arms, assistance, assistants, audible capacity, bargain, brokers, brothers, capability to withstand, chest, co born, comforts, communication, communication aids, communication methods, communication systems, companions, compassion, competitions, confidential things, correspondence, courage, cousins, dreams, ears, ear ailments, ear rings, environments, fights, firmness, foot, friends, hands, harmonisation with others, help from others, heroism, hobbies, intelligence gained out of studies, interest in education, laboures, landed property, letters, library, likes and dislikes, literature, longevity of parents, mental disorders, memory, mentality, musical talent, neighbours, neighbourhood, nephews and cousins, nervous system, news agency, observing religious rites and customs, offering of libation to the manes, ornaments, patience, partition of property, patriotism, perseverance, physical fitness, post office, recreations, relatives, religious frenzy, reporters, right ear, roads, road side places, rumours, scapula, selfishness, servants, short travels, shoulders, signing of contracts and documents, slaves, small vehicles, sports, steadiness, strength, throat, upper regions of the chest, valour, vigour, wicked intention, writing, written material, younger brothers and sisters.

Fourth Bhava

Agriculture, ancestral house, ancestral properties, ancient places, ant hills, antiques, archeology, bed, boats, breasts, buildings, cattle, cemetery, character and conduct, cheating mentality, chest, cleverness, contentment, conveyances, cosmetics, cot, cow dung, cows, delicacy, domestic appliances, domestic surroundings, door, dress, drinks, educational status, education up to the college level, elbow joints, elephants, estates, father's longevity, fields, fishing ponds, friends, fountains, gardens, government jobs, grave yards, grief, groves, heart, hidden treasure, highway roads, hopes, horses, house, immovable properties, interest in studies, investments, landed assets, mansions, maternal relatives, marital pleasures, medical treatment to the children, memorial, milk, mines, Mother, monuments, native place, nephew, nests, oil bath, primary and basic education, perfumes, personal behaviour, private affairs, public buildings, rearing of pet animals like cow, deer, rabbits etc., red soil, religious symbols, relatives, residential place, ribs of the body, roadside, savings, seat, secrets, secret life, ships, sister's children, snake holes, step-father, stomach, sweet smell, tanks, termites, travels, vehicles of all sorts, wasps, water, water pump, wells, wet lands, wife's occupation.

Fifth Bhava

Affluence, ambassadors, amusements, aptitude, artistic talents, auspicious expressions, authority, authorship, backside of the human body, bad principles, belly, betting, character, charity, cheerfulness, children, competitions, conception, contentment, courtship, creative writing, crossword games, dedication, devotion, discretion, emotions, entertainments like cinema, dance, drama and musical concerts, erudition, fame, father, fortune, friendship, good conduct, good morals, gall bladder, gambling, grace of the God, grandfather, heart especially the right ventricle, hereditary, hobbies, horse race, impregnation, inclination, intelligence, intuition, Ishta Deiva, kidnap, king, legal and illegal pleasures, lottery, love, love affairs, literary pursuits and interests, liver, Mantra, memory, mental ability, mental inclination, mentality, messenger, minister ship, ministerial cabinet, nobility, paternal property, physical and mental happiness, playing of musical instruments, pregnancy, previous birth, proficiency in musical instruments, progeny, puzzle, race, rape, reasoning ability, recreational activities, religious hymns, romance, satiety, secrets, sobriety, scholarship, sculptor, society, social inclination, speculation, spiritual practices, spleen, sports, stock exchange, stomach, support the unknown, traditions, theatre, upper abdomen, Vedic chanting, Vedic teaching and learning, virtuous deeds, wisdom, worship, exercises.

Sixth Bhava

Accidents, agitation, allegations, anguish, appendicitis, bad habits, banks, battle, boils, borrowings, calamities, camel, cause of diseases, colicky pains, competitions, criminal activities, debts, digestion, disappointments, diseases of both mental and physical origin, diseases that can be cured, domestic animals, donkey, draughts, dysentery, employees, enemies, fear, food, forgetfulness, greed, humiliation, hunger, hygiene, illness, ill health, imprisonment, indifference with brothers, indulgence, injury due to animals or fire or weapons, insanity, kidney, large intestine, liabilities, litigation, loan, loss in court cases, lower abdomen, maternal uncle and aunt, miserliness, navel, notoriety, nursing care, obstacles, opposition, pain, pet animals, physical injury, poison, quarrel, recovery from diseases, servants, Service, shocking occurrences, slander, small business outlets, small pox, step mother, stomach ulcers, subordinates, superstitions, swellings erupting in the body, tenants, theft, the state of being stolen, thieves, thirst, throat disorders, tuberculosis, uncle, unhealthy, unnatural death or crisis either due to snakes or water or weapons, untimely food, vices, worries, wounds.

Seventh Bhava

Adultery, arguments, battle fields, bed rooms, business, business partner, business speculations, business tendencies, chastity, companionship, conjugal bliss, contracts, curd, delicious food and beverages, desire, details about the beauty, character, nature and qualities of the spouse, dhal varieties, diplomacy, disharmony with wife, disputed places, divorce, enemies, flowers, ghee, grandfather, kidneys, ladies living areas, legal battle, legal bond, legal sanction, life partner, litigation, loss of wife, lost articles, lust, marriage, marital life, music, name and fame in foreign countries, open enemies, opponent, ovaries, partnership, passion, perfumes, prostate glands, public contacts, public gatherings, public help, public interactions, quarrels, recovery of lost wealth, renal system, secret enemies, secret love affairs, semen, seminal vesicles, sexually acquired diseases, sexual act, sex partner, social customs, spouse, success in love affair, swooning, talent, time of marriage, travels, triumph over enemies, ups and downs of the marital life, vision, wars, Maraka sthana.

The first marriage, the second child are denoted by the 7th house.

Eighth Bhava

Accidents, bonus payments, brothers' enemies, calamities, capital punishment, cause, nature and place of death, cervices, chronic diseases, conspiracy, conspirators, corruption, death by drowning, defeat, delay, degradation, detective stories, detention, deviation from accepted norms, difficulties, disagreements with the spouse, disappointments, discontinuance, disgrace, dishonour, disruptions, dowry, failures, father's debts and misfortunes, external genital organs, fall, fear from enemies, fire, gratuity, happiness, hidden treasure, hindrance, hostel, ill reputation, impediments, imprisonment, incurable diseases, inheritance, insults, insurance, investments, journeys through difficult terrain or mountainous areas, killing of animals, laziness, legacy, longevity, loss of body parts, lottery, mental agony, misfortunes, money lending, never-ending diseases or worries, obstacles, occult practices, operation theatres, parting away of friends or partners, pelvis, pension, pre mature death, private parts, quarrels, religious conflicts, robbery, scandal, secondary sexual features, separation, servants, spouse's wealth, strife, suicide, testicles, toilets, traitor, travelling across the rivers or seas, unearned wealth, unexpected financial gains as well as losses, urinary diseases, uterus, vagrant life, will, worries.

In a female's horoscope this house denotes her husband's longevity.

Ninth Bhava

Association with good people, brother in law, chanting or/and initiation of Mantras or Vedas, charity, clarity of mind, compassion, construction of temples or temple tanks or other such divine deeds, Coronation, counselors, cows, devotion, distant places, dreams, dutiful, divinity, educational laurels, efforts to pursue education, elephants, faith, fame, familial customs, far away news, forethought, fortunes, Father, godliness, good luck, goodness, grand children, Guru, higher education, hip region, holy places, holy baths, horses, intuition, knees, lakes, lawful, long distance travels, loyalty, marriage halls, medicines, meditation, merits of previous life, monastery, monetary circulation, morality, participation in virtuous deeds, paternal property, penance, philanthropy, philosophy, pilgrimage, preceptor, precious gemstones, proficiency in epic stories and in propagating them, religion, public service, public welfare, publishing books, religious activities, religious rites and rituals, religious inclination, religious institutions, research, respect to elders and gods, righteousness, sacrifice, science, sons and daughters, spiritual initiation, sympathetic tendencies, teacher, temples, thighs, virtuous deeds, vision, voyage in the air and sea, water sheds, wells, wife's brother, wisdom, worship.

The second marriage is indicated by this bhava as it is the 3rd from the 7th house, the house of first marriage.

Tenth Bhava

Advancement, agriculture, ambitions, aristocracy, assemblies, authority, awards and rewards, business ability, business enterprise, business mind, ceremonies, command, construction of towns, death rites done to ones' parents, defence status of the country, desires, devotion, dignity, elevation, employment, fame, father's wealth, father's longevity, favourites, foreign trips, fortune, government service, government quarters, government recognitions, government transport, hidden treasures, highest positions in the Government, honour, inns, judges, knees, knee caps, leaders of various associations, means of livelihood, name and fame, nature of job, occupation, permanent income, permanent job, pilgrimage, political clout, position, power, prestige, profession, proficiency, progress, prominence, promotion, public esteem, public life, royal seal, recognition, refugees, reputation, respect, renunciation, royal favour, sacrificing mentality, skeleton of the human body, sophisticated vehicles, status, successful undertakings, superiority, support, temples, teaching proficiency, titles, trading activities, worship, yoga.

The occupation or the profession is denoted by this 10th house only. The second business is denoted by the 12th house as this is the 3rd from the 10th house.

Eleventh Bhava

Accumulation of wealth, acquaintances, advisors, ancestral property, ankles, arrival, aspirations, awards, blood circulation, brother in law, colleagues, daughter in law, elder brother, elder sister, expenditures, foreign assignments, foreign collaborations, foreleg, friends, flatters, fulfillment of all desires and objectives and expectations, gain, gains through in laws, gold, left ear, left hand, legal affairs, mode of income, mother's longevity, nature of income, paramour, paternal uncle, possession of horses and elephants, profits, prosperity, rewards, recognitions, religious deeds, right foot, supporters, sea voyage, vehicles, well-wishers, wishes.

Twelfth Bhava

Accidents, air crash, air travels, anguish, banishment, change from one's native or permanent place of residence, comforts of the sleep, confinement, cunningness, conversion to another religion, death, death of the spouse, defective or mutilated limbs, diseases of the feet, disputes, distant travel, donations, drudgery, emigration, enemy's threats, end of one's life and attaining salvation (Moksha), exile, expenses, expenses on charity, extra marital life, extravagance, fall, feet, food, fraud, handicapped persons, heaven, hell, helping tendency, property by inheritance, hospitalization, hurdles in marriage, illness, inadequacy in sexual life, impediments, imprisonment, intoxicants, investments, left eye, life after death, limitations, litigation, living in abroad, losses, loss of body parts, loss of job, loss of position, loss of spouse, lost things or persons or property or wealth, malice, mental asylum, misfortune, murder, needless animosity, nursing homes, occult practices, persecution, poverty, public apathy, punishment, relief from debts, renunciation, repayment of loans, revengeful, sacrifices, sanatorium, secret acts, secret enemies, sedition, self-undoing, serving or living in abroad, separation, sexual intercourse, seclusion, sleep, sleeplessness, solitude, sorrow, sinful deeds, suicide, superstitions, suspicion, tribulations, waste, wireless communication, wounds.

Case Studies

The theoretical part of the Jamakkol prasanam is dealt in detail so far and now the practical applications are explained by way of case studies. Usually, in the Prasanam methods, the answer to the queries are simple, straight and to the point. It may be many a times a "Yes" or No" or similar such one liners only. This is true with the Jamakkol prasanam techniques also. But in all the case studies given here a lot of effort and time is taken to describe the logic and astrological principles and rules behind those answers. But in practice, the answers will be precise, perfect and sharper.

Case Study 1

Which is my family deity?

The family deity is the particular God which is being worshipped by a family and/or by a group of their relatives' families. Each individual family has a deity of its own. Many families have the same God as their family deity also.

The family deity is worshipped as per the family customs. It is customary to worship the family deity as the first and the foremost. During the eve of special occasions like marriage, or construction of a new house, or at the commencement of new business ventures, or at the time of physical ailments, special prayers are being offered at the family deity temples. Usually these temples are situated in the native villages where their ancestors lived long ago. In the present scenario many people have moved to urban cities or even abroad and they have lost touch to their roots. Some of them forget which is their family deity or its location. Some worship the wrong ones. In the pursuit of searching for the family deity, the people consult the astrologers. Every astrologer today is facing this query in his day to day professional life at least from fifty percent of his clients. The family deity can be identified in numerous methods in astrology. Here we will see how Jamakkol prasanam helps to identify the family deity, otherwise known as, the Kula deiva.

Date	26/10/2003
Time	18 34 hrs.
Place	Tiruppur
Tamil date	Iyppasi 9
Day	Sunday
Sex	Male
Age	35
Udhayam	Thula
Aarudam	Thula
Kavippu	Rishaba
Planet in the Udhayam	Bhudha
Planet in the 10th house	Sani
Planet affected by Kavippu	Chandra

Mercury	Jupiter		Mars
	Kavippu		
Rahu		Kavippu	Sun
Venus		Ketu, Sat	
Sun, Ven	Jup, Mars, Merc, Moon	Udhayam	Aarudam
Saturn		Moon	Snake

To find out the Kula deiva, find out the status of the Udhaya, the 5th and the 9th houses. Here the 9th lord Mercury is found debilitated in the outside and inside it has combined with the Mars, Mercury and the debilitated Moon. The 5th lord Saturn is placed in the bhadaha house, Simha, along with the Ketu. Both inside and outside, the Saturn is transiting towards its exalted house, the Libra. The udhaya adhipathi Venus is with the bhadaha adhipathi Sun. All these confirmed that their Kula deiva is forgotten for a long time and not worshipped. Now the 10th lord Moon is outside the Udhayam and has moved out of its debilitated house. Whenever there is an involvement of Moon either inside or outside the Udhaya, then there will be relief assured to the client. And that relief will come at the earliest possible.

The combination of the Mercury in a Female sign with the strong Mars, the Jupiter and the debilitated Moon indicated that their Kula deiva is Vishnu Durga Devi. The Mercury indicated the Vishnu connection and the Mars, the Durga devi. The deity would be simple without much decorations. The Moon indicated the female deities without much of decorations. Here the Moon is debilitated. So it was told that the Deity would be kept in an isolated place in a temple where regular Poojas are performed. Whenever there is the involvement of the planet Guru, the Poojas will be conducted in regular and proper ways.

Based on the Rasmi value of the Thula udhayam (2) and the Moon (21) there, the distance was told to be around 23 kilometers south of their native place. The Udhaya adhipathi Venus is in the Makara rasi, which indicates the direction as the South. The client left satisfactorily with the available information and in a week's time he returned after successfully visiting the Deity. The distance was 25 kilometers and all our other descriptions remained the same.

The rasmi is thus used to calculate the distance in this illustration.

Case Study 2

Which is my family deity.

A stranger came to my office and straight away told that he has come to find out his family deity. A Jamakkol chart was prepared and the Udhayam is placed in the Mesha, the Aarudam in the Dhanus and the Kavippu in the Simha. The connection of 1,5 and the 9th house indicted that the native is earnestly searching to find out his Kula deiva.

The 10th lord Saturn is in the 3rd house with the Mercury outside. The Kavippu is in the 5th house which indicates the family deity and also the ancestors. The Kavippu also indicated the worship of the family deity has been discontinued. The Kavippu affects the Guru placed there, which is the 9th lord also. The Jama graha Guru was exalted in the 4th house. The 3rd lord Mercury is in the retrograde state in the 5th house.

So whatever the details regarding the Kula deiva available with him are inadequate.

Date	11/09/2003
Time	13 42 hrs.
Place	Thanjavur
Tamil date	Aavani 25
Day	Thursday
Sex	Male
Age	35
Udhayam	Mesha
Aarudam	Dhanus
Kavippu	Simha
Planet in the Udhayam	Rahu inside and Sukra outside
Planet in the 10th house	Moon outside
Planet affected by Kavippu	Guru

Saturn	Venus		Mercury
Moon	Udhaya Rahu		Sat
Mars*			Jupiter
Moon		Kavippu Sun Merc* Jup	
Aarudam		Ketu	Venus
Snake		Sun	Mars

The Aarudam indicates the past events. The Aaruda adhipathi Guru is in the Simha with the Sun and the retrograde Mars. In the 5th house Rahu is present. The 5th lord is also present in the 10th house from the Aarudam as the Jama graha. In the gochara the Mars is present in the Kumbha as retrograde. The Mars denotes the weapons and the fire. The Venus in the 5th house denotes the female deities. The Simha denotes the hilly places. The retrograde Mercury represented a god which may have distorted appearance or look. The retrograde Mars also indicates the abnormality.

The Rahu in the Udhaya indicates the animals like the dog or the horses. The Venus in the Jama graha confirms the dog. Combining all these above factors, I told him his Kula deiva is a Male deity with a leg or hand deformed and carrying weapons in the hand and with a dog by its side. The temple will be located in a raised placed. The Mars is placed in the sign of Saturn. So the name of the god will be Karuppu (black) Sami. Since the Mars in the Kumbha gets the aspect of the three planets the Sun, the Jupiter and the retrograde Mercury from the Simha rasi, three other deities will also be present in the same campus. One of them being the Guru will be worshipped according to tradition and other three gods including the main deity will be worshipped with animal sacrifice. The combine aspect of the Mars and the Saturn on the Leo indicted the sacrifice of the animals. The deity is seen riding a horse and going for hunting with weapons in hand two dogs beside him. Everything suited perfectly to the Jamakkol description, thank God.

The Mars is in the sign of Aquarius or Kumbha rasi. This sign represents the month of Maasi according to the Tamil calendar. It is roughly between the 14th of February to the 4th of March. I told him the name of his Kula deiva is Maasi Karuppana Sami. Anna means the elder brother and the aspect of the Jupiter gave this name, This God is worshipped in the part of south Tamilnadu and it is well known. Immediately, the client told he knows that place and some of his relatives also are worshipping it as their family deity too. I confirmed it that it is the same God for him also. He left satisfied. After a month, he informed me over phone that he visited the temple along with his family and offered his prayers. He said after the visit to the deity he felt much relieved and some of his problems got melting down, thanks to the Jamakkol prasanam.

Case Study 3

What is the cause of the death?

Date. 19/12/2006   Sun rise 06 36 am
Time. 15 59 38   Sun set 05 58 pm
Place. Tiruppur

The client came and asked to find out the cause of the death of his relative. The death happened in abnormal situations he told further.

The Udhayam is placed in the Thula and the Aarudam in the Meena rasi. The Kavippu is placed in the Makara the 4th house. The 10th house Kataka is occupied by the Sun. Since the question is about the past event, the Aarudam is analysed. The Mandhi is located in the Aaruda rasi itself which confirmed the question about the death. The Mercury is placed as the Jama graha in the debilitated state. The Mercury is the bhadaha adhipathi for this Aaruda. The 10th house is occupied by the Sun and the Venus and the Saturn as the Jama graha. The Sun is the 6th lord and the Venus is the 8th lord and the Saturn is the 12th lord from the Aarudam. The Dhanus is a fiery sign. Combining all these facts, I declared that the death must have happened in the house due to fire. The third lord Venus is present in the 10th house. The third house denotes self-involvement among so many karakas. So the person must have self-immolated himself and died in the hospital. The 12th lord Saturn and the Rahu in the 12th house indicated the hospital stay.

When seen from the Udhaya also, the bhadaha adhipathi and the fiery planet Sun is placed in the 10th house, Kataka as the Jama graha. This is the 4th house of the Kaala Purusha indicating the house. The tenth lord Moon is in the debilitated state,

What is the significance of the Kavippu here? The Kavippu is placed in the 4th to the Udhaya and the 11th to the Aaruda. It affects the Saturn, the 11th and the 12th lord. It indicates the reason for the self-immolation. The problem with the ancestral property (Saturn as the

4th and the 5th lord) with his elder brother (Saturn as 11th and 12th lord) has made him to come to this hasty and foolish decision. The Kavippu is in the star of Uthrashada, the star of the Sun which is the 6th lord to the Aaruda indicating the involvement of the litigation.

Date	19/12/2006
Time	15 59 hrs.
Place	Tiruppur
Tamil date	Markazhi 4
Day	Tuesday
Sex	Male
Age	45
Udhayam	Thula
Aarudam	Meena
Kavippu	Makara
Planet in the Udhayam	Chandra in the outside
Planet in the 10th house	Surya
Planet affected by Kavippu	Moon

Mercury		Jupiter		Mars
	Aarudam Mandhi			
	Rahu			Sun
Venus	Kavippu		Ketu Saturn	
	Sun Venus	Moon, Jup, Mars, Merc	Udhayam	
Saturn			Moon	Snake

Case Study 4

Which is my correct horoscope.

A client came with four horoscopes and asked me which one among them was right. He told me that in the three horoscopes it was day time birth and in the fourth horoscope it was noted as night time birth. He asked me to find out which one is correct among the four. I did not touch his horoscopes but prepared a Jamakkol chart to find out the truth.

In the chart, the Udhaya is the Kumbha, the Aaruda is the Kanya and the Kavippu is in the Virschika rasi. The Sun is also placed in the

Virschika rasi and the Kavippu touches it. Since the Kavippu affects the Sun, the day time lord, it itself is indicated that the birth was in the night only. The outer Sun is placed in the 8th house to the udhaya. It was further confirmed by the Kumbha Udhaya which is the sign of the Saturn which is the Karaka for the darkness and the night.

Then I looked at the horoscopes. Only one horoscope which is for the night time birth had the Kumbha lagna. The Jamakkol prasanam has precisely spotted it. I want to cross check the chart. I asked him whether he has younger brothers. He said that his younger brother died when he was young. Why this was asked is, the 3rd house denotes younger coborn. The 3rd house lord from the udhaya was the Mars and it was found debilitated in the outer square. The Mandhi and the 6th lord Moon were also present in the 3rd House Mesha.

The 3rd house from the Aaruda was also Virschika and the lord again the same Mars. Moreover, the Kavippu is also present in the 3rd house here. It indicates the absence of the younger coborn. The lagna lord Saturn is in the 12th house to the Udhaya. The 12th house indicates distant places and the Saturn indicates the father's younger brother. Here being the udhaya adhipathi, the Saturn indicates the client also. So I told him you must be working in a foreign country and your father's younger brother must be also working in a foreign country. He replied with full astonishment, that both of them were working in the same place in abroad. He left satisfied for having his doubt cleared.

But, again he came after 10 days and asked whether the same question can be checked again. Silently, I put the Jamakkol chart and the Udhaya was today in the Thula rasi with the Saturn placed exalted there itself. The Thula rasi was trine to the previous Kumbha udhaya. On that day the Udhaya was in the star of the Pooratadhi and today it was in the star of Vishaka. The client said his 20 years of doubt has been cleared that day.

Date	26/10/2003
Time	18 34 hrs.
Place	Tiruppur
Tamil date	Iyppasi 9
Day	Sunday
Sex	Male
Age	35
Udhayam	Kumbha
Aarudam	Simha
Kavippu	Virschika
Planet in the Udhayam	Bhudha
Planet in the 10th house	Sani
Planet affected by Kavippu	Surya

Venus	Mercury		Jupiter
Rahu	Mars / Moon / Mandhi		
Udhaya			Sat * Mars
Saturn Venus			
	Kavippu / Sun / Merc	Jupiter	Aarudam / Ketu
Moon		Snake	Sun

Case Study 5

Deity details.

The question from the client was that he was worshipping a particular deity and whether that deity would fulfil his prayers. The Snake was in the Udhaya and the Rahu in the Aarudam and the Kavippu was in the star of Ardra.

Date	08/09/2009
Time	10.37.00 hrs.
Place	Tiruppur
Tamil date	Aavani 23
Day	Sunday
Sex	Male
Age	29
Udhayam	Makara
Aarudam	Virschika
Kavippu	Mithuna
Planet in the Udhayam	Chandra inside and Snake outside
Planet in the 10th house	Mars outside
Planet affected by Kavippu	Venus outside and Mars inside

| Jupiter | | Mars | | | | Sun |

Mercury

Snake

Venus Saturn Moon

Case Study 6

Job for the brother.

The question asked by a client. Will my brother get a job in any government organization?

Date	03/09/2007
Time	08 43 46
Place	Tiruppur
Tamil date	Aavani 17
Day	Monday
Sex	Male
Age	30
Udhayam	Libra
Aarudam	Sagittarius
Kavippu	Aquarius
Planet in the Udhayam	Sun outside
Planet in the 10th house	Jupiter
Planet affected by Kavippu	Moon

The Government is indicated by the Sun. It is found that the Kaaraka planet, the Sun is in its debilitated form in the Udhaya lagna in the Jama graha. The Udhaya was in the sign of the Libra which itself has declared the result as Negative. But, we will go in to the Prasanna chart how this result is indicated by the Jamakkol prasanam. Then only we can identify why he was denied of the government job.

The 10th house is occupied by the exalted Jupiter. The Jupiter is the Karaka for the 3rd and the 6th house. So job (6th house) for the brother (3rd house) has been rightly indicated. But the 10th house lord, the Moon is affected by the Kavippu.

The Sun is placed in the inside square in the Leo with the combination of Ketu and the Saturn. The Saturn indicate the delay and the Ketu the denial. Moreover, the Leo is the Bhadaha house for the Libra udhaya. The Kavippu is in the 5th house, Aquarius and its lord the Saturn is with the Sun and the Ketu. The Ketu denotes the Legal problems and the Saturn is the lord of the seventh house for the Leo. So I told the client that there must be a problem in that. The client then hesitatingly admitted that there is a police case against his brother for eloping with a minor girl in the name of love.

The retrograde Venus, the 5th house Kavippu, the Saturn – Ketu combination with the Sun all indicated the love affair and the consequent legal hurdle. The placement of the Udhaya and the Aaruda in the 3/11 position is a good augury, but, here it only indicted that his brother is qualified for the post. The rest of the arrangements clearly specified that he is not destined to covet the job in government sector as his legal problems are not easy to get resolved.

Saturn	Venus		Mercury
	Kavippu	Ven(R)	Jupiter
Moon		Sun Ketu Sat	
	Aarudam	Udhayam	
Snake	Sun		Mars

Case Study 7

When will he come?

It often happens in all our daily lives. We will be waiting for someone and when it gets delayed, we tend to ask whether he will come or not and if he is coming when will he arrive.

There is a method in Jamakkol prasanam to find an answer to this question. When there is the Moon in the outside or in the inside of the Udhaya or in the seventh house from it, the particular person has not started from his place yet. If there is the Moon in trine to the Udhaya in the inside or the outside, it indicates that the person is on the way and may reach at any time.

One day when I was at my office, a friend asked me whether I can tell him at what time the client who has taken my appointment for consultation would come. Half an hour has passed from his appointment time and after meeting him we had a plan to go out. So my friend was curious to know when the client would come.

Date	08/02/2006
Time	18 45 hrs.
Place	Trichy
Tamil date	Thai 26
Day	Wednesday
Sex	Male
Age	39
Udhayam	Aquarius
Aarudam	Sagittarius
Kavippu	Leo
Planet in the Udhayam	Bhudha
Planet in the 10th house	Moon
Planet affected by Kavippu	Sun

The Moon in the Mithuna rasi is placed in trine to the Udhaya lagan, the Kumbha. So according to the rule, the person is on the way to meet us very soon. The expected time is calculated using the Rasmi values. The Moon is in the Libra now. And when the Jama graha Moon reaches the Leo, it will be trine to the Aaruda and that time the event of his coming will happen. Additionally, it would be in the Nivarthi sthana of the Aquarius udhaya. Now the time taken by the Moon to reach the Leo has to be calculated. The value of the Rasmi is used for this.

The time of the question	18 45hrs.

The rasmi for the Moon is 21. It has to cross the Libra and the Virgo to reach the Leo.

For Libra 21 and for Virgo 21 Rasmi. Adding them with the time of the question,

18 45 + 00 42 = 19 27 hrs.

The expected person will come at this time. I calculated like this and write it on a paper and gave it to my friend. We waited and at last, the expected person came exactly at 19 hours 27 minutes. There is a Parivardhana involving the Guru and the Sukra in the chart. The person wanted to come and meet me first and go to a textile shop. Instead, he visited the shop first and came to my appointment delayed. The Venus is the Kaaraka for the textiles and the Jupiter for astrological guru.

The usefulness of the rasmi can be inferred from this example.

Mercury	Jupiter		Mars
Rahu		Mars	Moon
Udhayam Mercury			Sat• / Sun
Mercury / Sun			Kavippu
Aarudam Venus		Jupiter	Ketu
Sat		Moon	Snake

Case Study 8

Wedding or work?

A man of about sixty years came with his daughter's horoscope and asked me when she would get married. The placement of the Udhaya and the Aaruda in the 1/7 position confirmed the question was about the marriage.

Date	04/01/2004
Time	17 07 hrs.
Place	Tiruppur
Tamil date	Markazhi 20
Day	Sunday
Sex	Male
Age	60
Udhayam	Virschika
Aarudam	Rishaba
Kavippu	Dhanus
Planet in the Udhayam	No planet
Planet in the 10th house	Jupiter retrograde
Planet affected by Kavippu	Venus

Mars	Sun		Snake
Mars	Rahu	Aarudam Moon Mandhi	Sat •
			Moon
Jupiter	Venus	04/01/2004 17 07 hrs Tiruppur	Jup•
Kavippu Sun Merc•	Udhayam	Ketu	
Mercury		Venus	Saturn

The placement of the Kavippu in the Kudumbha sthana, the 2nd house indicated that the time is not yet ripe for the marriage. Whenever the Kavippu is present in the 2nd house it prevents the entry of the new member in the family be it the spouse or the child. The bhadaha adhipathi Moon is found exalted in the 7th house and also strongly placed in its own house in the Jama graha arrangement. The Mandhi is also present there. The 2nd lord Guru is debilated in the outer square. The 7th lord Venus is moving towards its debilitated house in the Jamakkol arrangement. The 10th lord Sun is in its exalted state in the 6th house. The Kavippu in the Dhanus is next going to affect the Venus in the outer square. Incidentally the Venus is the 7th lord for this Scorpio udhayam. All these parameters indicated that the marriage is going to get delayed.

Moreover, they denote about profession only and none of them is connected to the marital life. The answer given to the gentleman was that his daughter is interested in her job only at that time and after few years only she would give her consent for the marriage. He then told me that her daughter is adamant that she would get marry only after her promotion in the job. The exalted state of the 10th lord confirmed this.

Case Study 9

Job in hand or in Job hunt

Date	15/07/2003
Time	17 41 hrs.
Place	Tiruppur
Tamil date	Aani 31
Day	Tuesday
Sex	Male
Age	23
Udhayam	Rishaba
Aarudam	Dhanus
Kavippu	Kanya
Planet in the Udhayam	Rahu
Planet in the 10th house	Mars
Planet affected by Kavippu	Moon

The young man asked me when he would get a job. The 10th lord Saturn is exalted in the 6th house from the Udhaya. The 7th cum 12th lord Mars is placed in the 10th house. The Rahu is located in the Rishaba Udhaya. The 10th lord Saturn is placed in the 2nd house along with the Sun and the lagna lord Venus. I asked him that already he was doing his own business which is indicated by the powerful Saturn and the 10th house placement of the Mars. Then, why he is asking about a job now. He told me there was a crisis and stagnation in his business and that is the reason he wanted to change over to a job leaving his business. The Rahu in the

Udhaya indicated his precarious situation. The Kavippu is in the 10th house to the Aaruda which will tell about his past, which showed that he was presently in trouble related to his profession. But why this situation? The seventh lord Mars is placed in the 12th house outside. So he must have faced the loss in his business due to his friends or partners. He nodded in agreement. The 6/8 placement of the udhaya and the Aaruda does not indicate favourable reply to his search for a job.

The combination of the Saturn with the Venus will give good returns of income if one puts hard work. They are placed here in the Dhana sthana, the Mithuna. So if he again starts his old business, this time without partners, he would get succeed. So instead of searching for a job, he could better go back to his former profession, I told him. The Kavippu in the 5th house also indicated that in his mind he was also not interested in a job but wanted to do own business only.

Jupiter	Mars		Sun
	Udhaya Rahu	Ven, Sat, Sun	
Mars		Jup Merc	Snake
Mercury / Moon			
Aarudam	Ketu	Kavippu	
Venus	Saturn		Moon

Case Study 10

Welcome child.

A client came and asked me whether he would beget a child. He was childless for more than 10 years. The Aarudam is placed in the 5th house to the Udhaya and this confirmed the question asked by the client. The Udhaya adhipathi Mercury was in the 10th house Kanya in a strong placement and the 5th lord Saturn was inside. The Aaruda adhipathi was the Saturn. The Saturn indicated the delay in progeny.

The 7th lord Jupiter was exalted in the 11th house. The fifth lord Saturn was in the 7th house outside. This is the house of Nivarthi sthana and also it was the house of the Puthra kaaraka Jupiter. This confirms the chances of the man getting a child. Moreover, whenever the Snake was involved with the Udhayam and be in the houses of 1,4,5 or 9 from the Udhaya, it indicates that the pregnancy and childbirth was assured. This is the golden rule in the Jamakkol prasanam in matters of progeny. Here the Snake was in the fourth house and so it was also in the house of the Jupiter. The Moon was in the Aaruda and the Jupiter was in 7th place to it. The Kavippu was in the 12th house to the Aaruda. The Aaruda refers to the female. These confirmed that the position in the female also assured the possibility of getting a child.

I told him that he would get a child definitely and even at that time his wife might be conceived. I asked him to go and test for the confirmation.

He felt happy and at the same time skeptical also about the prediction and also on the possibility that his wife may be pregnant at that time. He left. After 10 days he phoned and in the enthusiastic voice informed that his wife was confirmed as pregnant. But her health condition needed complete medical care, he further informed.

Whenever the planet in the Udhaya or in the 10th house is associated with 3rd or 8th house, the native needs medical care. Here the Mars, the

3rd and 8th house lord and the kaaraka for the medicine was present in the Udhaya.

The Kavippu was in the fourth house. The Kavippu indicates a secret or a hidden thing. Here it concealed the pregnancy. But it was indicated by astrology which was confirmed by the doctors later.

Date	18/08/2003
Time	19 50 00 IST
Place	Coimbatore
Tamil date	Aavani 1
Day	Monday
Sex	Male
Age	36
Udhayam	Kanya
Aarudam	Makara
Kavippu	Dhanus
Planet in the Udhayam	Mars outside
Planet in the 10th house	Mercury outside and Saturn inside
Planet affected by the Kavippu	

Saturn	Venus		Mercury
Mandhi	Moon	Rahu	Saturn
Mars*			Jup, Sun Mer, Ven / Jupiter
Moon / Aarudam			
Kavippu	Ketu		Udhayam
Snake		Sun	Mars

Case Study 11

Perils of love.

A young lady came to my office and told me that she wanted to have Prasanam done for her. She has heard of it and has come from a long distance to consult me. I put the Jamakkol prasanam chart.

The seventh lord Guru was in the Udhaya and the 7th place was occupied by the exalted Sukra. The Sun was outside the Udhaya. The Udhaya adhipathi Bhudha was in the 3rd house in the inside and 8th in the outside. The tenth house was also occupied outside by the 7th lord Guru. So the query must be regarding her 7th house only. Now watch the Aarudam. The Aarudam is used to indicate the past happenings. The Udhayam was placed in the 5th house from the Aarudam. The fifth house denotes the Love. So instead of marital life I took the love as her question. The Bhudha is the kaaraka for the love. The Udhaya adhipathi Bhudha was with the Rahu in the 8th house. In the inside the Bhudha was placed in the 3rd house along with the Mars and the Venus in the 3rd house. The 3rd house indicates sexual indulgence. The Rahu indicates shadowy activities. Already the Venus was in the exalted state. The Sun is the planet for the imagination. He is also placed in the Udhaya. Combining these factors, I told her that she is in an illicit relation with a married guy. The 5th house is aspected by both the Saturn and the Mars indicating that the love will not get success. Since the 7th lord is in the Udhaya she is having lot of imagination about her love and the so called lover. But, for the Kanya udhaya the 7th house is the bhadaha house and any time the love will get break up, I told her. When the Udhaya adhipathi is in combination with the Rahu or the Ketu, wrong deeds continue and right things will not be continued. Here the Bhudha is the Udhaya adhipathi and he is with the Rahu and going towards his debilitated house. So I cautioned her, that she will have to face disgrace and trouble and advised her to discontinue her illegal affair. The Kavippu in the 2nd house is against the formation of a family life for her. The planet Mars which indicates the husbands in female chart is in its debilitated house here.

Date	23/12/2004
Time	15 08 IST
Place	Coimbatore
Tamil date	Markazhi 6
Day	Thursday
Sex	Female
Age	28
Udhayam	Kanya
Aarudam	Rishaba
Kavippu	Thula
Planet in the Udhayam	Guru inside and Surya outside
Planet in the 10th house	Guru
Planet affected by Kavippu	Sun

Venus	Mercury		Jupiter
	Rahu	Aarudam Moon	
Mandhi			Saturn	Mars
Saturn			
Sun	Mars, Venus, Merc,	Ketu, Kavippu	Udhaya Jupiter
Moon		Snake	Sun

Case Study 12

What is missing?

The person asked me to find out what was missing from his house and the reason for it.

The Kavippu was in the 8th house to both the Udhaya and the Aaruda. So the question about something missing was correctly indicated. Whenever anything is lost or missing, the 8th house or its lord will be connected to the Udhaya or the Udhaya adhipathi or the Aaruda or Aaruda adhipathi or to the Kavippu. This is the golden rule in the matters of missing objects and stolen things or lost persons.

The 10th lord from the Udhaya was the Moon and it is placed in the 9th house, outside. The 9th lord Bhudha is placed both inside and outside of the Udhaya. The Kavippu was in the star Kirthikai, the star of the Sun. The Sun denotes the father. So I asked the client whether his father was missing. He confirmed it and asked about his present status. I said he was safe and would return in the next few days. The udhaya adhipathi Sukra is strong in his own house, indicating the safety of his father. The Udhaya was in the Movable sign. So I told him that his father was travelling somewhere at that time. The Bhudha is placed in the inside of the Udhaya. And in the outside of the Udhaya it has engaged in a Parivardhana with the Venus, thereby the Venus gaining strength in its own house. So I told him during the day when the star of the Venus was present next he would return.

The reason for his leaving the house was again indicated by the Bhudha. The Bhudha denotes younger co-born and also it was the Kaaraka for love and lovers. I told him that his father was not happy with the love affairs of his daughter and so left the house. The Sun, the Kaaraka for the father was debilitated in the udhaya and the udhaya is surrounded by 5 planets. These showed the confused mentality and the helpless state of the father who had no other go except to leave the house. The planet in the 10th house was Saturn. The Saturn is the 4th and the 5th lord for this Udhayam. So the Saturn indicated that the reason for missing must be his children, the 5th bhava kaaraka. The love is also indicated by the same 5th bhava. He nodded in the affirmative. Later, after few days he phoned that his father had returned home safe. The star on that day was Poorvashada, the star of the Venus.

Date	26/10/2003
Time	18 34 hrs.
Place	Tiruppur
Tamil date	Iyppasi 9
Day	Sunday
Sex	Male
Age	35
Udhayam	Thula
Aarudam	Thula
Kavippu	Rishaba
Planet in the Udhayam	Bhudha
Planet in the 10th house	Sani
Planet affected by Kavippu	Chandra

Sun	Snake		Moon
	Rahu, Asc	Kavippu	Sat • Mandhi
Mars			Saturn
Mars			Jup
		Udhayam, Mer, Sun, Ketu, Ven, Moon	
Jupiter		Mercury	Venus

Case Study 13

Son or Sin?

The lady came with a query regarding her family dispute. She wanted to find out the reason and the remedy for the quarrel. The Udhaya and the Aaruda were in the 1 – 7 position. The 10th lord Mars is placed in the 2nd house. The 6th lord Moon was in the 10th house. All these indicated the rift between the husband and the wife. The Udhaya lord Saturn was placed in the Mithuna, the 5th house in the inside and in the Dhanus in the outside. The Kavippu was present in the Dhanus which was 5th from the Aaruda sign. The Sun and the Saturn were present there. The combination of the Sun and the Saturn indicates delay or denial of a child. The fifth lord Bhudha is nearing the Udhaya. The 5th lord Bhudha was in the debilitated state. The Mars and the Saturn placed in the 5th house also showed the obstructions in child bearing.

Considering all of these I told her that it was regarding the child. The childlessness was the reason for their fight. The lady nodded yes and asked further if her plan could succeed. I analysed the chart to find out her intention. There was an exchange of the Sun and the Jupiter in the chart. This is 1/ 5 exchange from the Aaruda and the 7/11 exchange from the Udhaya. Combining these I told her that she wanted to change her husband and ready to bear a child with some other man. And chances were very high that her mission to get a child would succeed. The Udhaya indicates the male and the Aaruda the female in the Jamakkol prasanam. Both the inside and outside Venus were 12th to the Udhaya. This indicated that the marital life was going to suffer. The 9th house indicates the second marriage. Here the Jupiter was present at the 9th from the Aaruda. So I advised her to go for legal process of separation and get a solemnized re- marriage and not to venture into any illegitimate ways. That kind of activities would land her in problems, both ethically and socially, I warned.

Date	09/01/2004
Time	20 23 IST
Place	Tiruppur
Tamil date	Markazhi 25
Day	Friday
Sex	Female
Age	36
Udhayam	Kumbha
Aarudam	Simha
Kavippu	Dhanus
Planet in the Udhayam	Bhudha
Planet in the 10th house	Chandra
Planet affected by Kavippu	Sukra

Mercury	Jupiter		Mars
Mars	Rahu		Sat •
Udhaya			Moon · Sun
Venus · Venus			Jup• Aarudam
Merc Sun Kavippu		Ketu	
Saturn		Moon	Snake

Case Study 14

Wife's woes.

A man came and asked about his wife's illness. He has not told me what was the problem but asked me whether she would become alright.

The Aarudam is at the 6th house from the udhaya indicating that this prasanam chart is about a disease. The Udhaya lagna is Thula and the Guru is outside it. The Guru represents the muscular organs in the body. The 10th house is occupied by the Moon which denotes the bladder like organs in the human body. Already, the Venus and the Ketu are present in the Udhaya inside also with the debilitated Sun. Combining all these, I asked him whether his wife is suffering from the uterine disorders. The Thula rasi also is the kaaraka for the uterus. The client told yes and further asked me when she would get cured. The Kavippu in the 3rd house and the aspect of the Saturn on the 3rd house and the placement of the Mars also there indicated that the physical contact between the husband and the wife is affected. The Snake in the Aarudam indicated that the problem started when she underwent an abortion. The Snake and the 12th house of the Kaala Purusha indicted the loss. The fifth house is occupied by a male planet Mars and aspected by the Guru indicated that the couple have two male children.

Analysing the planetary states, the Moon is well placed in the 7th and the 10th houses. So remedy is possible. When the Moon reaches the Udhaya the lady will become alright. For that the Moon has to cross the 7 squares. Using the rasmi value of the Moon, 7 X 21 = 147. This should not be taken as 147 days. Since the Moon takes roughly one month to travel the zodiac, it is to be taken as month and 5 days. So the lady will get cured in a months' time.

Date	20/10/2003
Time	17 58 IST
Place	Tiruppur
Tamil date	Iyppasi 3
Day	Monday
Sex	Male
Age	40
Udhayam	Thula
Aarudam	Meena
Kavippu	Dhanus
Planet in the Udhayam	Guru outside
Planet in the 10th house	Sukra outside and Sukra, Surya and Ketu inside
Planet affected by Kavippu	Guru

Snake	Moon	Sat
Aarudam / Rahu		Sat
Mars		Moon / Venus
Sun		Jupiter
Kavippu	Sun, Ven Ketu Udhayam	Mercury
Mars	Jupiter	Mercury

Case Study 15

Loan – to take or not?

A person came from Tanjore and put his query directly. He has problems in his business and the loans have mounted huge. He wanted to get rid of them by pledging his landed property but no one came forward to take it. At last one gentleman approached him and was ready to pay the money he required. But, at the same time some people warned our client that the lender was not a good man and he resembled the Shylock in matters of loan. Now our client's question was should he get a loan from him or not.

I answered him after analysing the Jamakkol prasanam chart that the lender would behave worse if his offer for loan was accepted. The reason for this answer the 10th lord Venus was exalted in the 8th H. The 6th lord and the kaaraka for the loans, the Saturn was placed in the Udhayam itself. The Udhaya adhipathi Sun was placed in the 10th house along with the Venus and the retrograde Mercury.

In this chart, the Kavippu was also placed in the Simha along with the sixth lord Saturn. This itself has indicted the heavy loan incurred by him and the subsequent ignominy he had to undergo.

Date	02/06/2008
Time	09 01 18 IST
Place	Tiruppur
Tamil date	Vaikasi 20
Day	Monday
Sex	Male
Age	54
Udhayam	Simha
Aarudam	Mesha
Kavippu	Simha
Planet in the Udhayam	Saturn inside and Sun outside
Planet in the 10th house	Mercury in retrograde, Sun and Venus inside
Planet affected by Kavippu	Mars

The 10th lord Venus is in the 8th house in the exalted state. The Venus denotes the money. So as soon as the person gives the loan amount he would disgrace the client, I told him. I advised him not to take his loan. But, the client who was desperate for money, was hesitant to take my suggestion. Then I told him, if he was not believing my words, he can first take a small amount from and test his genuineness and motive. He agreed to this proposal and went back. After a month he came back and told that the lender behaved exactly what has been described. Even for a small amount of the initial loan he has put various strict conditions which are difficult to comply with. Now for this small loan itself the client is feeling the heat.

From this chart, many things can be learnt. The Udhaya lord, the Sun was placed in the 10th house. It shows the loan that had acquired by the client is only for his business needs and not for anything else. The Mercury is retrograde in the inside and in the Jama graha the Mercury is going towards its debilitated house. The Mercury is the 2nd and the 11th lord for this Udhaya indicating the Dhana sthana and also the Labha sthana. Moreover, the Mercury, is the Kaaraka for the documents, the agreements, the negotiations, the instalments etc., When the Mercury is placed weakly in as chart, naturally its Kaaraka will get affected. The deal will not be fair and proper. This is the golden rule indicated by an affected Mercury. The Jupiter is the 5th and the 8th lord. The Jupiter is retrograde in the 5th house and as the 8th lord it is placed in the 11th house outside. The placement in the 8th H again indicates a disgrace in waiting. So its position is also not helpful to the client. The Yoga Kaaraka Mars for this Simha lagna is found debilitated both inside and outside the Kataka and also placed in combination with the Ketu. It indicates, the police (Mars) and the legal (Ketu) involvement may follow soon. The Rahu is placed in the Makara with the Saturn outside of it. Though the Saturn is well placed in its own house, the combination of the Rahu indicates the crisis in his business. The Rahu is the planet for mortgage and pawn broking. Its placement in the chart in the 6th house clearly shows the situation of mortgaging the land for the money. Please remember, the Makara is an Earth sign.

Venus	Mercury		Jupiter
	Moon Aarudam	Merc*, Sun, Venus	
			Ketu Mars / Mars
Saturn / Rahu		Saturn Udhaya Kavippu	
	Guru*		
Moon		Snake	Sun

Case Study 16

Can I sign?

A young man of 30 years came and asked whether he can be a surety for his uncle (father's younger brother) who was taking a big loan to manage the financial loss in his business. If we say yes, then we allow all the procedures that follow the signing of the surety papers, the young man told me. Rather warned me.

The Udhaya was in the Kumbha rasi and along with that the Rahu and the 3rd house lord Mars were present. The Jupiter was moving towards the Udhaya at the outside. Whenever there is either the snake or the Rahu involved with the Udhaya, it means that the native is going to face severe crisis. Here unfortunately both the Rahu and the inimical planet to it, the Mars were connected to the Udhaya. So there was an imminent fall waiting for him. The father's younger brother is denoted by the Saturn. Here the Jama graha Saturn was in the 9th house in the Libra in the exalted state. It might appear stronger, but, it is the bhadaha house for the Kumbha udhaya lagna. The Bhudha is the planet for the documents, surety, bank, agent, middle men etc., Here the Mercury is in its debilitated house in the 2nd house to the Udhaya. The Jama graha Mercury is in the 12th house. The 6th lord Moon is in the 8th house, indicating the disgrace he had to face because of the loans. The 2nd and the 11th lord Jupiter, the indicator of Dhana and the Labha is in the retrograde state in the 10th house. The Jama graha Guru is getting affected by the Kavippu. Already the Guru is at 344 degrees in the Kumbha rasi and moving towards its debilitated house of the Makara. The 7th house is the house of Nivarthi sthana. Here it is the Simha. But, neither the sign nor its lord Sun is in the favourable aspect of the Guru. So I warned the young gentleman not to sign the surety for his uncle.

The client did not listen to my counsel and he signed the papers. The uncle got the loan but failed to repay the amount. As a result, the young man had to abscond from his house unable to face the debtors. Above all, the Kavippu in the 2nd house has simply told the whole story.

The reason for the financial loss was not asked by the client, when he met me for the second time. But it was clearly indicated by the Prasanam. The udhaya adhipathi Saturn in the retrograde state in the 6th house with the Jama graha Snake has indicated the illegal and unethical business and the character of his uncle, which has ruined the business. The rules of the prasanam say that the astrologer should give his answers only for the questions that were asked. So I kept silent.

Date	17/04/2001
Time	17 01 hrs
Place	Tiruppur
Tamil date	Chitrai 4
Day	Tuesday
Sex	Male
Age	30
Udhayam	Kumbha
Aarudam	Mesha
Kavippu	Meena
Planet in the Udhayam	Rahu and Mars
Planet in the 10th house	Guru in retrograde state inside
Planet affected by Kavippu	Guru

Guru	Mars		Sun
Kavippu Mercury	Moon, Sun Aarudam	Venus	
Mercury			Saturn• — Snake
			Ketu
Venus	Jupiter•	Saturn	Moon

Case Study 17

What Am I?

A man of forty years asked me the question. What is the present condition of my life and what is the future? He has not told his problem. Whether it is personal, professional, financial or health etc., So his problem and the solution have to be found out from the Jamakkol prasanam. Accordingly, the chart was prepared for that time.

The Udhaya was in the Meena and the Aaruda in the Kanya. The Udhaya adhipathi Jupiter was well placed in the 10th house in the outer square as the Jama graha. The 2nd lord Mars was exalted in the 11th house Makara. So finance could not be a problem. Next I saw the Kavippu to find the answer. The Kavippu was in the Thula. The Kavippu was in the 8th house which indicated bad situation only to the native. But what is that?

The 6th lord Sun was in the Udhaya and it indicated legal cases, loans or ill health. The Venus was in exchange with the Mercury and this exchange was taking place in the 7th and the 8th houses. The Kavippu was in touch with the Venus now. The Udhaya and the Aaruda were in the 1/7 position and this indicated that it could be a problem with husband and the wife. So I asked him if his wife was not living with him. He confirmed it and asked what would happen to them. Moreover, the placement of the Kavippu in the7th H of the Kaala Purusha denoted the family problem.

The Venus is with the Ketu in the Simha which is the 6th house. The Venus is also in the retrograde state and the 12th lord Saturn is also present there. So the wife is not averse to the idea of getting divorced and separated by the legal process. I explained this clearly to the client.

In the Jamakkol prasanam the Udhaya refers to the male and the Aaruda the female. So I told him the Sun was in the Udhaya and because of false prestige issues, he had fought with his wife. Whenever the Sun was in the Udhaya it indicated the issues of pride and prestige. Since the Snake was moving towards the Udhaya next, it would bring him crisis like court cases. The Snake is going to engulf the Udhaya which is nothing but the native in this chart. So it was advised to him that it was better on his part to talk to his wife and bring her back. The Jupiter was aspecting the Udhaya and so his wife would be ready to come along with him, if invited. The parivardhana also symbolises the displacement from one place to another and so his wife would also like to move from her place. Otherwise, the 6th lord Sun in the Udhaya would go in for legal procedures. The udhaya adhipathi and the 10th lord Jupiter is found in the retrograde state in the 9th house, Virschika. The retrograde state shows that the client is not able to look forward about the future. He is dwelling in his mind on the past happenings and thereby decides against the continuation of marriage life.

Moreover, there is a parivardhana of the outer Saturn with the inner Moon. The Moon indicates the mother and if he goes to his wife's house with his mother and talk to her she will definitely oblige. The Moon in its own star, Shravan, is strong in the 11th house indicting his mother is capable enough to solve the issue.

He left half-heartedly. After a months' time he came to my office with his wife. He told if I had not cited about the legal troubles he would not have invited his wife. The reason for their separation has not told by the client or his wife. Upon analysis of the chart it has been found that both the Udhaya adhipathi (the husband) and the Aaruda adhipathi (the wife) are well placed in the chart. But the 6th lord Sun in the Udhaya and the 8th H placement of the Kavippu gave the answer that because of his debts and the subsequent dishonour to his name and to his family, angered the wife who has left him. I advised him to be careful in his finances hereafter.

Date	30/07/2007
Time	15 27 hrs
Place	Tiruppur
Tamil date	Thai 24
Day	Saturday
Sex	Male
Age	45
Udhayam	Meena
Aarudam	Kanya
Kavippu	Kavippu
Planet in the Udhayam	Sun
Planet in the 10th house	Guru
Planet affected by Kavippu	Sukra

Sun	Snake		Moon
Udhaya		Mars	Mercury
Rahu		Sun	Mercury
Mars / Moon		Saturn Venus* Ketu	
	Jupiter*	Kavippu	Aaruda
Jupiter		Mercury	Venus

Case Study 18

When will I get the loan?

	02/05/2008
Time	09 35 hrs.
Place	Tiruppur
Tamil date	Chitra 20
Day	Friday
Sex	Male
Age	50
Udhayam	Simha
Aarudam	Thula
Kavippu	Kumbha
Planet in the Udhayam	Saturn
Planet in the 10th house	Mercury
Planet affected by Kavippu	Mercury

A person came and asked whether he would get the loan he has applied for purchasing the land. And if yes when he would get it. These were his questions.

The Aaruda was in the fourth house from the Udhaya. The 4th house denotes immovable properties like house, lands etc., The 10th house was occupied by the Bhudha which indicated the vacant lands. So his question was confirmed. The 10th lord Sukra, the karaka for money was in the 5th house, the Dhanus. So his mind (5th house) was about the money. Since the Jupiter is also placed in the 5th H, I told him that he would definitely get the loan amount and the loan would be released in the month of Aani (15th June to 14th July), when the Sun travels in the Mithuna rasi.

The Saturn was in the Udhaya. The Saturn was the Kaaraka for the loans and here he was also the 6th lord indicating loans. So the Saturn has given him the thought about the loan. The Udhaya adhipathi Sun was exalted in the Mesha along with Venus inside and the Mars outside. The Jama graha Sun or the outside Sun was in the Mithuna, the

11th house to the Udhaya. So his plan to go in for a loan would get succeed definitely. When the transit Sun enters the 11th house Mithuna his loan would get sanctioned. This was the basis for the reply given to him.

The Kavippu is placed in the 7th H. He asked me whether he can take the loan from his friends or purchase the land combined with him. I told him the 7th H Kavippu does not allow the involvement of the friends or the partners and warned against it. Moreover, the Kavippu affects the Mercury which is the planet for cooperation and coordination. So I told him to go alone in his pursuit.

Since the Saturn was in the retrograde state in the Simha Udhaya, it was told to him that there would be a change in the expected money value or the expected time of it. He again came after 3 months and informed that he got the sanction order as soon as the Sun entered the Mithuna. But the money was released only after a month.

Jupiter		Mars		Sun
	Moon	Sun, Venus	Mercury	
	Kavippu		Ketu Mars	Snake
Mercury	Rahu		Sat* Udhaya	
	Jupiter	Aarudam		
Venus		Saturn		Moon

Case Study 19

Searching the son

This is about a missing person. The client has told that his son was missing. Where was he and when he would return were his questions.

The 8th lord Venus was exalted in the Udhaya. Whenever there is a connection between the Udhaya and the 8th house or its lord or there was connection between the 10th house and the 8th house or its lord, the prasanam indicates something or someone is missing. So the question about the missing person has been indicated.

Date	28/06/2007
Time 12 28 hrs.	15 54 hrs.
Place Trichy	Trichy
Tamil date Aadi 5	Aani
Day	Thursday
Sex	Male
Age	56
Udhayam Makara	Meena
Aarudam Kanya	Kumbha
Kavippu Simha	Rishaba
Planet in the Udhayam Snake	Venus inside
Planet in the 10th house Mars	Moon outside
Planet affected by Kavippu Mercury	Mercury

1. The 8th lord Venus is in the Udhaya. So the person is missing. The exalted Venus indicates pleasures and enjoyment as one of its karakas.

2. The Kavippu is placed in the 3rd H. The third house is the house of communication and also it indicates short travels. Since this house has been afflicted by the Kavippu, the person is not nearby. Secondly, there is no possibility of immediately getting any information about his whereabouts.

3. The 10th house is occupied by the 5th lord Moon outside it. And the Moon and the Guru are combined in the 9th house. As the 5th lord, the Moon denotes love among so many kaarakathuvas. And whenever the Moon and the Jupiter are combined it also shows elopement and secret matters. These natives with this combination in their charts, either they cheat others or they get cheated by the others. The activity depends on the strength and the placement of them in the chart.

4. The 5th house is occupied by the Venus and the Saturn inside and the debilitated Mars outside.

5. The 7th lord Mercury is travelling towards the udhaya which is also its debilitated house.

6. The Aarudam placed in the 12th H also indicates the long distance travel.

Combining all these factors, I told my client that his son is safe and he must have gone to a faraway place with a girl. The return of the missing persons will be indicated by the 2nd, 7th and the 11th houses. Here the 7th lord Mercury is in the 2nd H. So there is 100 percent possibility that his son would return safe. But the 11th lord is Saturn and it would delay his return.

The Udhayam and the udhaya lord are both in the Upaya (Common) houses. And in the Jamakkol prasanam whenever an event happens in the Upaya rasis, it will recur once again. It is a golden rule. I asked whether the same thing has happened before and the dejected father told yes.

Case Study 20

Money theft

There was a phone from a big organisation in our town and they asked me if I could come to their office immediately. They told me it was about a missing object and they wanted the whole thing confidential. I did not go there, but I put a Jamakkol prasanam for that moment and answered.

Date	21/07/2011
Time	12 28 hrs.
Place	Trichy
Tamil date	Aadi 5
Day	Thursday
Sex	Male
Age	50
Udhayam	Makara
Aarudam	Kanya
Kavippu	Simha
Planet in the Udhayam	Snake
Planet in the 10th house	Mars
Planet affected by Kavippu	Mercury

The Kavippu is placed in the 8th place from the Makara Udhaya and this confirmed that there is something went missing. The Udhaya adhipathi Saturn is debilitated in the 4th house Mesha. The Mercury was present outside the Kataka and inside the Simha where the Kavippu is also placed. The Sukra is placed in the Mithuna which is the 6th house both inside and the outside.

It is an educational institution which is confirmed by the Kanya Aaruda and the presence of the Jupiter there. The 10th house is occupied by the 4th and the 11th lord Mars. The Guru was present in the Aaruda and the Guru denotes the money. The Guru denotes the money of bigger value and the Sukra denotes smaller value. To put it simply, the Guru denotes the money in the bank and the Sukra indicates the money in the wallet. Since the Guru in the Aarudam indicated the money, I asked if any money is lost. They confirmed it and asked if I can find out how much is lost and who could be the thief. They said it was the admission time and the donation amount collected by them was unaccounted and they do not know how much is lost. And they suspect a person and whether he was the culprit.

Using the rasmi value, the value for Makara is 8 and for the Snake in it is 4. The Udhaya adhipathi Saturn is debilitated and so no value for it. So I concluded that the value should be 1. 2 lakhs. Regarding the person who must have stolen the amount, there is a rule in the Jamakkol prasanam that the planet in the Kavippu will indicate the thief. Applying this, here the Mercury is the planet in the Kavippu and therefore it indicates the Accountants and I passed the information to them. They replied that the amount could be more or less correct and they are also suspecting the accountant only. The Sun is in the 7th sthana. Whenever, the Sun is present in the Nivarthi sthana, the thief could be identified. The Sun sheds light on the darker areas.

Since the Udhaya lord, the Saturn is debilitated, the school authorities are not in a position to give a police complaint as the money involved is the black money.

Moon		Saturn				Venus
	Moon	Jupiter	Mars Ketu	Venus		
					Sun	Mercury
Snake	Udhaya			Kavippu Mercury		
		Rahu		Aarudam Saturn		
Sun			Mars			Jupiter

Case Study 21

Money – Missing or stolen?

Date	19/08/2000
Time	16 48 hrs.
Place	Tiruppur
Tamil date	Aavani 3
Day	Saturday
Sex	Female
Age	45
Udhayam	Mithuna
Aarudam	Makara
Kavippu	Kanya
Planet in the Udhayam	Sukra outside. Rahu inside
Planet in the 10th house	Moon both outside and inside
Planet affected by Kavippu	Bhudha

A lady came with a query about a missing thing from her house. The Udhaya represents the querist. The 8th house indicated the missing things or the persons. Here the Aaruda is placed 8th from the Udhaya. So it has specified that it was a prasanam about a missing object or person. The Venus was placed outside the Udhaya and so it showed that it was the money that was found missing. We have not taken the other kaaraka of the Venus, since the Venus was placed in the house of Bhudha indicated the cash (paper currency). The lady also confirmed it. (the Sukra - wealth and the Bhudha - Paper). The money kept by her in the Amirah is missing.

Since it was told missing from the house, the fourth house was analysed and the Guru was placed there. Moreover, the 4th lord and the lagna adhipathi Bhudha was found nearing the Udhaya. So I told her that the money has not been lost and it was kept safe in some other place by someone in the family. May be she herself has placed the money in some other place and searching here, I told. But, she confirmed that it was her usual place to keep the money. Since the Kanya rasi indicated book shelves, I told her to search in books and paper stands. The Venus in the Udhaya is also the fifth lord. So I advised her to enquire her children also.

The rasmi value for the Moon is 21. The Moon is placed 10th from the Udhaya. So we calculated the rasmi value as 21 x10 = 210. So I told her within the next 21 hours when would get her money back. While applying rasmi values we have to apply the logic and our common sense in determining the time period. Of course, by experience it can be mastered. Because here we cannot say 21 days or even 2 days and so we told just 21 hours only. Because the money is lost inside the house only, it could be searched by that time.

Later in the day, that lady phoned and informed that her son has kept the money in his cupboard. She has not asked if he has stolen it or just kept the money for safety in his cupboard. In the 10th house, both the Moon were present. We have cited in many instances, that the Moon indicates craftiness and dishonesty. So something fishy has happened with the son which the client does not want to elaborate and we also kept quiet and not bothered. The money was restored in full.

Whenever there is Sun in the 7th house, the Nivarthi sthana, the thief is caught in theft prasanam. When the 6th or the 10th lord is debilitated, the thief will not be able to enjoy his loot. Here the 6th lord Mars was found weakened in the Kataka.

Moon	Saturn	Venus
Moon	Jupiter	Udhaya Rahu
		Mars / Mercury
Snake / Aarudam		Sun, Ven Merc
Ketu		Kavippu
Sun	Mars	Jupiter

Case Study 22

Daughter's distress

What is the health problem for my daughter and when it will get cured?

This is the question asked by a father who is aged around 50. He wanted to know about his daughter's health.

The Mars is the planet moving towards the Udhayam and the Guru has just crossed the udhayam. The Mars is the 5th lord indicating the question is about his child. But the Mars is getting debilitated when it reaches the Udhaya. So this confirms the health crisis of his daughter. The Guru in the Simha is getting exchanged with the Sun in the

Dhanus. The Guru thereby occupies the position of 6th in the inside and 12th in the outside to the udhaya. After applying the Parivardhana, now the Guru happens to be the 6th lord and in the company of the 3rd and the 12th lord Mercury and the Snake outside. When the Guru happens to be the 6th lord and the disease inflicting planet, it does not shun away from giving diseases, in spite of it being a benevolent planet. But it makes the diseases less painful and manageable by treatment.

The Snake was also present in the outer square of the Dhanus. Whenever the Snake is present it indicates abnormal and critical states. The Snake and the Rahu when they are related to the disease states, they act strange. The diseases denoted by them are either unidentifiable and they give an ugly look. This girl was suffering from a type of skin disorder and the skin peels out like the scales of a fish or the skin of a snake. The Mercury is responsible for skin diseases and the Guru manifested it in a bigger proportion. The Snake indicated the withering away of the skin. The Kavippu in the 11th position does not show any immediate relief. The Aarudam in the second house Simha and its lord Sun getting debilitated in the Libra and in the company of the Ketu indicated that the luster of the face and the skin of the girl is in a diminished state.

The Nivarthi sthana adhipathi Saturn is retrograde in the 12th house in the gochara and it is placed in the Meena rasi in the outer square. When the retrograde motion becomes normal there could be some relief and once when the outer Saturn reaches its houses the Aquarius and the Capricorn, major relief could be seen. This was my reply to the worried father. The Moon indicates medicinal plants and herbs and it is now placed in the Nivarthi sthana, the 7th house. So it was also advised to him that the treatment with herbs would bring cure for his daughter. The udhaya adhipathi Moon in the Nivarthi sthana indicated relief to the girl. The aspect of the Jupiter from the Simha on the 6th house also indicted positive outcome.

The 10th house is also occupied by the combination of Venus and the Rahu inside and outside. This also indicates the waning away of the sheen of the girl.

Date	30/12/2003
Time	13 25 hrs.
Place	Tiruppur
Tamil date	Markazhi 15
Day	Tuesday
Sex	Male
Age	50
Udhayam	Kataka
Aarudam	Simha
Kavippu	Rishaba
Planet in the Udhayam	Guru
Planet in the 10th house	Venus
Planet affected by Kavippu	Venus

Saturn		Venus		Mercury
	Moon Mars	Rahu	Kavippu	Sat*
			Udhayam	Jupiter
Moon	Ven		Aarudam Jupiter	
	Sun Merc*		Ketu	
Snake		Sun		Mars

Case Study 23

What is my position now?

Date	07/02/2004
Time	12 24 hrs.
Place	Tiruppur
Tamil date	Thai 24
Day	Saturday
Sex	Male
Age	48
Udhayam	Kataka
Aarudam	Simha
Kavippu	Rishaba
Planet in the Udhayam	Moon
Planet in the 10th house	Sun in the outer square
Planet affected by Kavippu	Sun

This person came and gave his horoscope and asked me simply to tell about his present position. The tenth lord Sun is in the exalted state. The Sun is the 2nd house lord also. So his source of income must be through government only. The udhaya and the Aaruda are in the 2-12 position which is not a good sign. Moreover, the Kavippu in the 11th house indicates that the native is living a life without any gains. The Jupiter is in the debilitated state in the Capricorn. Combining all these factors, I told him the following. He is employed in a government sector. The 10th house Mesha is ruled by the Mars and it is a movable sign. This indicated that he is a driver in a government transport service wearing uniform. Now the Mars the lord of the 10th house of profession is with the Rahu inside indicating a disturbance. The Mars is in the 9th house outside which is the Vraya house to the tenth house of profession. So the problem is with his job. The 11th house placement of the Kavippu indicated the negative or adverse reply to his query, whatever it may be. The planet in the Udhaya is the Moon. Whenever there is a Moon in the Udhaya, the questions are asked about the native himself. The Moon also indicated a certain amount of depreciation and deceit. And finally, the results are happening very soon. Here both the Saturn aspected the Mars. In conclusion the situation is such that he might lose his job. Now he opened his mouth and told that any time he might be terminated because of an accident he had committed. And yes, he has no progeny. His wife is sick (indicated by the Venus and the Ketu combination in the Libra). His house is also in a litigation denoted by the presence of the Venus and the Ketu in the 4th house. He was particularly anxious about his job, but, the planets indicated that it is going to be over soon. The Kavippu is going to engulf the 10th house and the Sun there in the outside. So his profession is going to be end soon and his financial position is getting in a turmoil. After hearing all this, he left speechless.

All his problems are indicated by a single chart.

Mars		Sun		Snake
	Ven	Mars Rahu	Kavippu	Sat•
				Udhayam	Jupiter
Jupiter	Mer Sun			Aarudam Jupiter
			Ketu	
Mercury			Venus	Saturn

Case Studies regarding marriages.

The Jamakkol prasanam comes very handy in matters of deciding the marriage matching. The astrologers are consulted frequently for the analysis regarding the matching of the charts for the marriage. Even some astrologers say it is a cash cow bringing in some money to the astrologer daily. The rules used in Jamakkol prasanam for the matters regarding marriage are:

1. The Udhayam denotes the male and the Aarudam denotes the female in the Jamakkol chart.

2. The Kavippu as usual denotes the hidden things and the secrets and also the hindrances in the marriage process.

3. In the matters of matching of charts, in the Jamakkol chart erected for the purpose, the Udhayam and the Aarudam should not be in the position of 6th or 8th or 12th teach other.

4. While analysing the two horoscopes for a marriage matching process, if a Jamakkol chart is constructed at that instant, many things regarding the matching can be inferred. The chart will give various details on the matching and also on the subsequent marriage.

5. If the Mercury is placed in the Udhaya or in the 10th house, that is a good time to check the matching and the probability of them are agreeing is very high. At the same time, the analysis for matching during the Jamam when the Bhudha is found in its debilitated house Meena is not recommended. Many a times, the proposal will not go through.

6. When the Mars is placed in the Udhaya or in the 10th H, the chance of getting them married is very high. Similarly, when the Venus is in the Udhaya of in the 10th H, the probability of getting married is very high. Because both the Mars and the Venus are Kalathra karakas.

7. In matters regarding the marriage, if the Udhaya and the Aaruda are placed in the positions of 1/7, then it is a good indication.

8. When the Kavippu is in the Udhaya then the male is not interested or he is not eligible or prepared for the marriage. When the Kavippu is in the Aaruda then similar thing can be said about the female.

9. When the Kavippu is in the 7th house to the Udhaya, the marriage proposal will be blocked by the boy's side. When the Kavippu is in the 7th H to the Aaruda, then the girl's side will reject the marriage proposal.

10. When the Kavippu is in the 2nd house to the Udhaya, then the marriage will not be held. As the 2nd house denotes the entry of a new person into the family, the Kavippu there delays or denies the event.

11. The position of the Kavippu with respect to the Udhaya in the various houses such as 3rd, 4th to 12th indicts different situations which might prevent the marriage. Similarly, the placement of different planets in the Udhaya indicate either the smooth conduct of the wedding or the stopping of it due to diverse reasons. These will be dealt in detail with suitable case studies in out next volume of the book on Jamakkol prasanam.

Case Study 24

When will I get married?

A young man of about 27 years consulted me regarding his marriage. His question is clear and direct. When will I get married. The placement of the Udhaya and the Aaruda in the 1/7 clearly showed that this prasanam is about the marriage proposal.

The planet in the Udhaya is the Bhudha and it is the 8th and 11th lord for this Virschika udhaya. The 11th indicates his desires, but the 8th ruler ship indicates hindrances. The placement of the Kavippu in the Kudumbha sthana is another negative indication. The Kudumbha sthana adhipathi, the Guru is found debilitated in the 3rd H. The 7th house is occupied by the Moon which is its exalted house and the Moon is the bhadaha adhipathi for this Udhaya. The kalathra planets like the Mars or the Venus is not connected with the Udhaya. All this indicated that the marriage is going to be delayed. But why?

The 10th lord Sun is found exalted in the 6th house. The Rahu is also present there. The 10th house is occupied by the retrograde Jupiter which is the 2nd and the 5th lord. This indicates that there is a problem regarding his family particularly his father. I told him this. He replied his father has pledged some of their family properties and so he wanted to recover them before conducting his son's marriage. Rahu is the planet for mortgage. The client told that it will take at least 2 to 3 years to settle the loans and then he gets married. But he came to consult me if there are earlier chances for marriage. I told him that the planets also indicate the delay. But the aspect of the Jupiter on the 2nd house and on the 6th house will ease out his repayment and hence the marriage also will be conducted soon.

Date	04/01/2004
Time	17 07 hrs.
Place	Trichy
Tamil date	Markazhi 20
Day	Sunday
Sex	Male
Age	27
Udhayam	Virschika
Aarudam	Rishaba
Kavippu	Dhanus
Planet in the Udhayam	Venus
Planet in the 10th house	Guru in the retrograde state
Planet affected by Kavippu	Bhudha

Mars	Sun		Snake
Mars	Rahu	Moon Aarudam	Saturn°
Ven			Jupiter° Moon
Jupiter			
Merc°, Sun Kavippu	Udhaya	Ketu	Saturn
Mercury		Venus	

Case Study 25

Will my daughter marry this boy?

A lady of about 50 years came with her daughter's horoscope and asked me the question directly. She wanted to know whether her daughter would marry her lover or she would listen to her parents who were against it.

The Jamakkol chart is put for that moment. The Udhaya is in the Mesha with the Guru inside and the Snake outside. The Aarudam is in the Meena with the Sun outside. The Kavippu is located in the Kataka with the Saturn also placed outside there. The Kavippu in the 4th house denotes the disagreement of the mother. The presence of the Guru in the udhaya itself has indicated that the marriage will be celebrated. But, since her mother is averse to this proposal we analysed why it is so. The Rahu in the Udhaya indicated that the boy is from some other religion. And that's the reason for her mother's objection. The mother also confirmed this when we asked and wanted to know whether it will happen or not.

The 5th lord Sun is in the 10th house inside and in the 12th house outside. So the mind of the girl is fixed on this marriage and even she would not hesitate even to elope with the boy. The Udhaya adhipathi is Mars is retrograde in the 5th and in the 10th house it is exalted outside. This shows that the girl is adamant about her love and also crooked in her mind and be ready to do anything for her love marriage. The presence of the Snake in the Udhaya and the Ketu in the second house indicates, that the marriage will face hurdles and problems. The Saturn in the 7th house inside is exalted and it shows that the boy is also equally adamant about the marriage.

The Saturn has engaged in a parivardhana with the Venus in the Aquarius. Similarly, the Mercury and the Venus in the 7th and the 6th houses are also in parivardhana state. This shows that the marriage (7) will go on as per their wish (11), but will also face difficulties (6).

The udhaya is strengthened by the presence of the Guru in it and the aspect of the Jama Guru from the Dhanus. The Udhaya adhipathi Mars is exalted. The 7th house is made stronger by the presence of the 10th and the 11th lord Saturn exalted. All these planetary arrangements will allow the marriage only, even if you like it or not. This is what I told the desperate mother and closed the consultation.

The Moon and the Ketu combination in the 2nd house denoted the mental stress experienced by the mother.

Date	02/02/2012
Time	09 55 hrs.
Place	Tiruppur
Tamil date	Thai 19
Day	Thursday
Sex	Female
Age	50
Udhayam	Mesha
Aarudam	Meena
Kavippu	Kataka
Planet in the Udhayam	Guru inside and the Snake outside
Planet in the 10th house	Mars outside and the Sun, Mercury inside
Planet affected by Kavippu	Saturn

Sun		Snake		Moon
	Udhaya Jupiter	Ketu Moon		
Venus			Kavippu	Saturn
Mars	Sun Mercury		Mars*	
	Rahu	Saturn		
Jupiter		Mercury		Venus

Case Study 26

Gullible groom

A client came and told that many horoscopes were coming to him by way of the marriage proposal to his daughter and he wanted to conduct the marriage at the earliest. He then produced a horoscope of a boy and told it was sent by his own sister and all of them are interested in that. He wanted my opinion to proceed further. He seems to be made up his mind to go on, but, he came for this consultation also. The tone of his speech indicated that he merely wanted a yes from me.

I put the Jamakkol chart for this. The Udhaya is placed in the Kumbha and the Aarudam in the Mithuna. The Kavippu is in the 12th house,

Makara. The 10thhouse was occupied by the 6th lord Moon. Then I told the client, that this must have been married already or he must have been facing charges and cases regarding his marriage. So better to avoid this proposal. The father was shocked and he did not believe even a single word from me. He argued for a long time in favour of the alliance and finally left the place.

After 3 months he came back and told that the boy was facing criminal charges because of his registered marriage with his lover and has been arrested. He thanked me profusely for saving his daughter.

How we told about that guy?

1. The 10th lord Mars is debilitated in the 6th house and is placed along with the Ketu there. Moreover, it has exchanged its house with the 6th lord Moon which is also debilitated in the 10th house.

2. The placement of Kavippu in the 11th house along with the Snake indicates that the Udhaya is not going to affected by the deal.

3. The Kavippu afflicts the Sun which is the 7th lord.

4. The Saturn placed in the 7th is the 12th lord also.

5. The Kavippu and the Snake are placed in the 7th house to the Aarudam. The Aarudam indicates the female and this placement in the Kalathra sthana is against the marriage activities.

6. The 6th house is the 12th house of the Kalathra house and it is occupied the Mars and the Ketu.

7. The Mars denotes the husbands in the female charts and here it is debilitated and is found with the company of the Ketu in the 6th house. The outer Mars is also found in the 8th H.

8. The father has come for the consultation and here the Sun the Kaaraka for the father is in debilitated house and is further affected by the Kavippu.

9. Incidentally, the Sun is also the Kalathra sthana adhipathi and it is in an afflicted state.

10. The Guru, the 2nd and the 11th lord is strongly placed in the 6th H. This strengthens the karakas of the 6th H like court cases, litigation, police intervention etc.,

Date	21/05/2008
Time	16 13 hrs
Place	Tiruppur
Tamil date	Vaikasi 8
Day	Wednesday
Sex	Male
Age	55
Udhayam	Kumbha
Aarudam	Mithuna
Kavippu	Makara
Planet in the Udhayam	Saturn outside
Planet in the 10th house	Moon inside
Planet affected by the Kavippu	Sun

Saturn		Venus			Mercury
			Merc, Sun, Ven	Aarudam	
Udhayam				Ketu Mars	Jupiter
Moon	Rahu			Saturn	
Kavippu Jupiter*	Moon				
Snake			Sun		Mars

Case Study 27

Marriage – yes or no

A friend of mine asked me over phone that a girl's horoscope is matching with his brother's horoscope and they wanted to go to the see the girl. He said he wanted my guidance to proceed in this marital matter using Prasanam methods. Mere matching of the horoscopes is not enough for him. He wanted the confirmation using prasanam.

The Jamakkol chart is prepared and the Udhayam is in the Mithuna and the Aarudam in the Dhanus. The Kavippu is in the 5th house Thula. The Udhayam and the Aarudam are placed in the 1/7 position and this is a good setting for marital matters. The Udhaya adhipathi

Bhudha is moving towards the Udhayam and this is also a good omen. The planet in the Udhayam is the Kalathra kaaraka Venus and this is an auspicious arrangement again. The Aaruda adhipathi Jupiter is also in the Kanya rasi and moving towards its exalted house. Again this is also a correct position. The 10th house is occupied by the Moon which is the Kudumbha sthana adhipathi, thereby indicating the formation of a family. Nothing wrong so far.

Now the Kavippu is analysed. It is in the 5th house. When the udhayam and the Aarudam are placed in the position of 1/7 and when the Kavippu is placed in the 5th house, in matters of marriage, it indicates the love affairs. So is the love a problem here. Since I know my friend there is no such an issue with his brother. But the girl we do not know.

The Jupiter is the 7th lord and also the bhadaha adhipathi for the Mithuna Udhaya. So I just hinted my friend to discuss with the girl and if she has full consent only in the marriage he can accept the proposal. He seems to understand this and agreed to it. When his brother was discussing with her he has touched upon the topic of her love. The girl was in disbelief for a moment and later she accepted that she loved someone in her college days and it was now a forgotten one. It was nothing but a teenage infatuation and has not proceeded any further. She wondered how he came to know that because he is totally from a distant town. She clearly assured my friends brother that the so called love was not there in her mind now and never in future also The problem is settled and the marriage is conducted in a grand manner. Everything went on well.

Date	01/09/2012
Time	16 41 hrs
Place	Tiruppur
Tamil date	Aavani 16
Day	Saturday
Sex	Male
Age	30
Udhayam	Mithuna
Aarudam	Dhanus
Kavippu	Thula
Planet in the Udhayam	Sukra
Planet in the 10th house	Moon
Planet affected by Kavippu	Guru

Moon	Saturn		Venus
		Jupiter Ketu	Udhaya
Moon			Venus
			Mercury
Snake			Sun Merc
Aaruda	Rahu	Kavippu Saturn Mars	
Sun		Mars	Jupiter

The installation of bore well.

In my astrology practice using the Jamakkol prasanam two topics have earned me a lot of name and fame. The one is about missing things or the prasanam about the lost or stolen things or missing persons. The second one is regarding the erection of bore well and getting adequate water supply. Both these prasanam are very useful to the people. The success of the prediction can be immediately felt in these two prasanam. It gives the satisfaction to the astrologer and happiness to the clients. I intend to deal these two topic separately with more case study examples and explanations in the second volume of this book. But as a curtain raiser, I am giving this case study regarding the bore well installation. And of course the topic regarding child birth is yet another important one which will also find a major share in the next volume.

The factors responsible for adequate water supply. These are with reference to the Jamakkol prasanam charts.

1. The planets which denote copious amount of good quality of water supply are the Moon, the Venus and the Jupiter. These are called wet planets or watery planets.

2. The Mercury denotes the sufficient water, but, not excess.

3. The Sun, the Mars and the Saturn denote dry planets.

4. The Rahu, the Ketu and the Snake indicate water supply after hindrances and with lot of effort only.

5. The rasi where the Moon is situated denotes the place where there is abundant water supply.

6. The Udhayam denotes the fountain of water.

7. The Signs the Meena, the Mesha, the Kanni and the Thula are called Rishaba Veedhi signs in the Jamakkol prasanam. These signs are also called as Veli rasis. They indicate the under current or the stream of water lying underneath.

8. When the Udhaya falls in one of the Veli rasis and the Snake is also associated with it, then abundant water supply is assured.

9. When the dry planets like the Sun, the Mars or the Saturn is in the Udhaya, then there will not be water in that site. On the other hand, it might be a rocky terrain.

10. When the watery planets occupy the Udhayam, good amount water is fully guaranteed.

11. The depth of the bore well to be installed is calculated using the rasmi values. While calculating the depth, the practice and the common sense is needed. And in addition to it, the situation prevailing in that area has also to be borne in mind. 50 may indicate mere Fifty feet only near a river bed. In the inland it may be Five hundred feet also. In some places it may be One thousand five hundred feet also depth.

12. The Kavippu not only indicates the absence of water, but also, other disturbances like the delay in work, the rod getting broken, the disagreement in the cost of work and the wages, wrong place of installation, disturbances from the neighbours or the people nearby, the poor quality of the water, insufficient water supply, the mechanical faults, the electrical failures, the manual disturbances etc., These are all dependent on the placement of the Kavippu.

13. In the bore well prasanam, the directions of the rasis are very important to mark the places which are abundant in water.

I can write more and more on this bore well installation, but, I reserve those things for the succeeding book. I am herewith presenting a few case studies on this subject.

Case studies on Bore well erection and water supply.

Case Study 28

Nonstop supply

A farmer from the town of Udumalapet wanted to erect a bore well in his agricultural land and he consulted me. The Jamakkol chart showed the Udhayam in the Meena and the Aarudam in the Kanya rasi, The Kavippu was in the 8th house and it is affecting the Udhaya adhipathi and the 10th lord Guru. The udhayam is in the Veli rasi and generally the Meena rasi denotes the water house. Moreover, the watery planet Moon is present there outside. The Udhaya adhipathi Guru is placed in the Kanya and therefore the Udhaya gets the Moon and the Guru connection. So everything seems to be auspicious and indicated good water supply. I was not happy to mark this Prasanam for good water supply because of two things.

1. The Kavippu is going to engulf the Guru which is the Udhaya adhipathi.

2. The dry planet Sun is placed in the 10th house. Moreover, the Sun is the 6th lord for this Udhaya.

3. The second house is occupied by another dry planet Saturn which is in its Neecha house.

4. The gochara Sani was in the Kataka with Mandhi inside and the Mercury outside. The Mercury denotes optimum water supply only.

But the client was not ready to delay as he has already paid the advance amount for the bore well installation and so he wanted to start the work at the earliest. He does not want to wait for another prasanam to proceed. Accordingly, the work got progressed and after a few days he was lucky enough to get a sufficient amount of water supply from the new bore well. The water is also good in taste and he shared his happiness with me. He paid the bore well installation people well.

But, in the next month the water supply in his bore well began to get reduced and finally it stopped completely one day. The reason being, his neighbour dig a new bore well in his fields which affected the water supply. The Mercury is the bhadaha adhipathi for the Meena Udhaya and it is placed in the Kataka rasi outside. The Kataka rasi denotes the direction of North. So his neighbour put his new bore well in the northern side of our client's field and disrupted the water supply.

Now our client has to select a new place and restart the installation process from the scratch.

Date	17/06/2005
Time	15 29 hrs.
Place	Udumalapet
Tamil date	Aani 3
Day	Friday
Sex	Male
Age	41
Udhayam	Meena
Aarudam	Kanya
Kavippu	Thula
Planet in the Udhayam	Moon outside and Rahu – Mars inside
Planet in the 10th house	Sun
Planet affected by Kavippu	Guru

Moon		Saturn			Venus
	Udhaya Mars Rahu			Sun Venus Mercury	
	Moon			Saturn Mandhi	Mercury
Snake					
				Guru Ketu Aarudam Moon	
Sun			Mars		Jupiter

Case Study 29

Depth of the water and depth of knowledge.

This man from Madurai came and asked me how many feet he should dig to get good water supply. He has not asked whether he can install a bore well or whether he will get abundant water supply. He has directly asked how much deep he should go to get water. In Prasanam the question is more important and we have to concentrate on the question before going to answer it.

The rasmi values are used to calculate the depth. The rasmi of the Udhaya rasi plus the rami of the planets in the Udhayam plus the planet which indicated the water supply. This is calculated as follows.

The rasmi of the Meena rasi is 27. The rasmi value of the Mars is 8. Total of this 35. Now we have to apply the common sense. So it can be 35 or multiples of 35 depending on the place. I asked him the general trend in that area. He said it touches 400 feet. I told him above 350 feet he will get water. And finally he got the water at a depth of 352 feet.

One more additional information from this chart. The Udhaya adhipathi Guru is in the 6th H inside and in the 11th house outside. I asked him if he has taken a loan to dig the bore well and he replied that he did. The connection of the Kavippu to the 6th lord Sun also indicated this.

Date	16/05/2004
Time	16 55 hrs.
Place	Madurai
Tamil date	60
Day	Vaikasi 3
Sex	Sunday
Age	Male
Udhayam	Meena
Aarudam	Meena
Kavippu	Mesha
Planet in the Udhayam	Mars
Planet in the 10th house	Mercury
Planet affected by Kavippu	Sun

Moon		Sun			Snake
	Aarudam Udhayam	Rahu, Mercury, Moon Kavippu	Sun	Ven, Mars, Saturn	
					Moon
Jupiter				Jupiter	
Mercury			Venus		Saturn

Missing persons

The questions about the missing persons and the lost things are frequently asked. There are few things which go missing often. The first and the foremost is the Jwellery. Then comes the persons. People abscond or get lost. The lovers get eloped. The economic reasons, love, lust, failure in business or studies, dishonour etc., are some of the reasons why people go missing. Then cash, documents like passport, certificates, pass books, cheque books, vehicles, wallets, keys are some of the other things which are generally and frequently getting missed. Small children are either lost or someone abducts them for gains. The 6th house denotes the lost things. The 8th house denotes the missing as well as stolen things.

The first bhava or the lagna or the udhaya denotes the missing persons or stolen articles. It denotes the person who lost them or the querist.

The 2nd house denotes the direction towards which the missing person/object is going or has gone.

The 3rd house denotes the source from which information can be gathered about the missing persons or the stolen thing. The planet in the 3rd house gives the data about the missing thing or the person. If the Mercury is present there, then the publicity about the missing person through newspaper and posters will be very helpful. If Mars is present, immediately take the help of the police. *Here a word of caution to the astrologer. The astrologer should always advice his clients to lodge a complaint with the Police regarding the missing persons or stolen things, before he starts analysing their query. This will save him from unnecessary and avoidable hassles later.* If Venus is present, then find out if any lady is also found missing in the same locality. If the Saturn is present, the search through the servants will be helpful.

The 4th house refers to the distance involved. The astute astrologer with his acumen and experience can decide the distance in terms of meters or kilometers depending on the planets involved.

The 5th house denotes the mind of the missing person. Whether he is angry, sad, happy, worried etc.,

The 6th house denotes the status of the life of the native before missing.

The 7th house denotes the thieves who took the objects. In case of the persons, it denotes the accomplice of the absconder. It also denotes the recovery of the stolen articles and the return of the missing persons.

The 8th house denotes the reasons for the person running away.

The 9th house denotes the involvement of the out-siders or third persons in the event.

The 10th house denotes the motive of the missing person.

The 11th lord, if he is connected to the 2nd lord or the 2nd house, the object or the person will return safe.

The 12 lord denotes the losses due to the theft or the missing.

The object denoted by the planet present in the Udhaya.

1	The Sun	Gold ornaments which are circular in shape. Value less
2	The Jupiter	Gold ornaments which are of higher value
3`	The Venus	Silver objects. And young ladies
4	The Mercury	The documents

The Mars generally refers to the vehicles. When combined with the Venus, the Mars refers to the costly and luxury vehicles. In the combination with the Saturn, the Mars refers to the old and the condemned vehicles.

Case Study 30

This person came to my office and told me that he has come to meet me on the recommendations of a common friend. I welcomed him and told him that he has come to consult me regarding a lost object and that would be recovered within the next 3 days. He then replied me that he has not opened his mouth so far and how can I say that prediction. Then I told him to tell me the purpose of his visit. He replied that he has come regarding a missing object only. He was curious to know how I could tell this merely by seeing him. Was it any magic or face reading he wondered? I said it was the gift of the Jamakkol prasanam that I could infer this and it is not magic. It is a clear way of prediction using well established rules and procedure, I replied him.

How this prediction was made?

1. The Udhaya adhipathi Guru is in the 8th house, both inside and the outside Jama graha.

2. The Guru is the lord of the 10th house which exhibits his mind.

3. The Udhayam is flanked by two Snakes. The Rahu is placed inside and outside is situated the Jama graha Snake.

4. The 10th lord Jupiter is in exchange with the 8th lord Venus.

5. The 7th lord Mercury is placed in the 12th house. The Mercury denotes the Kalathra sthana adhipathi for the Meena udhaya.

6. The Mercury has entered in to an exchange with the Jama graha Saturn which is in the 4th house.

7. So I concluded that he must have lost his wife and has come to enquire about her whereabouts.

8. The Venus placed in the 10th house also confirmed this. The Venus denotes the wife in the male charts.

9. The 7th place is now occupied by the Ketu and this is waiting to get them separated for ever. The Ketu is a graha which cuts the bonds.

Date	12/02/2006
Time	08 10 hrs.
Place	Tiruppur
Tamil date	Thai 30
Day	Sunday
Sex	Male
Age	34
Udhayam	Meena
Aarudam	Mithuna
Kavippu	Meena
Planet in the Udhayam	Rahu inside, Snake outside
Planet in the 10th house	Venus inside, Mars outside
Planet affected by Kavippu	Moon

Now the question is why she is gone and where?

The Mars, the 2nd lord is in the 3rd house, the house of communication. So he has suspected his wife and that is the reason for her parting away from him. The Aarudam would indicate the past events. It is occupied by the Saturn which has gone on an exchange with the Mercury. The second house to the Aarudam is again occupied by the retrograde Saturn and Moon inside and the Venus in the Jama graha. The Aarudam is affected by the Saturn Mars combination. The Guru also aspect the Aarudam from the 8th house. So the husband's words must have hurt the wife and out of humiliation, she has left him.

But was she good? This question might seem unnecessary, but, for astrological purpose only we analyse all the possibilities in the chart. The 7th lord Mercury is in its own house in the inside and the Jama graha Bhudha is in its exalted state. These speak the impeccable character of the wife.

Where is she now? The 7th lord Mercury is in its own houses inside and in the Jama graha outside. So she must have gone to her parent's house only. The Mars is present in the 3rd and the 10th house. Therefore, if her brother is enquired about her, he would tell the truth. There is a mutual aspect of the Sun and the Saturn. Whenever there is a Sun and the Saturn connection in a female's horoscope she would be very affectionate towards her father. The same combination in a male's chart indicates the exact opposite result. Here there will not be cordiality between the father and the son. Here the wife who is attached with her father has gone to him and he has given her shelter.

The Jama graha Chandra will reach the Udhaya rasi in the next 2 or 3 days. So the husband would be able to get some information about her in the next 3 days. I warned him about the impending danger from the Ketu in the 7th house. After a week or so, he came to my office again, this time with his wife. He said he got a clarity after the last week's consultation and so went to her house and brought her back. All is well and that ends well.

Snake	Moon		Saturn
Udhayam Kavippu Rahu		Mars	
Mercury			Sat* Moon / Venus
Sun / Sun			
	Venus	Jupiter	Ketu
Mars		Jupiter	Mercury

Timing of Events

The fixation of timing of fructification of results needs practice and also it should be situation oriented.

1. When the Karaka and the bhavaha meet at the Udhaya lagna.

2. When the Moon touches the Udhaya lagna (use the Rasmi or rays of the Moon to calculate the time interval). When yearly planets like the Guru, the Sani or the Rahu and the Ketu treat the time period in years. The Mars, the Sun and the Venus indicates months. The Mercury indicates the weeks. The Moon indicates the days.

3. When the Udhaya adhipathi gains strength by way of exaltation, ownership or conjoin with benefics.

4. A weak Udhaya adhipathi indicates that the native is not equipped with the necessary qualification to get the expected results. He does not possess the requisite conditions to fulfil his aim.

Appendix 1

Tamil months Equivalents Zodiac sign

1. Chitra April 13/14 to May 14/15 Mesha

2. Vaikasi May 15/16 to June14/15 Rishaba

3. Aani June 15/16 to July 16/17 Mithuna

4. Aadi July 17/18 to August 16/17 Kataka

5. Aavani August 17/18 to September 17/16 Simha

6. Purattasi September 16/17 to October 16/17 Kanya

7. Iyppasi October 17/18 to November 15/16 Thula

8. Karthikai November 16/17 to December 15/16 Virschika

9. Markazhi December 16/17 to January 14/15 Dhanus

10. Thai January15/16 to February12/13 Makara

11. Maasi February 13/14 to March14/15 Kumbha

12. Panguni March15/16 to April113/14 Meena

Appendix 2

There is a basic difference in the way the horoscope charts are written in the South Indian method and the North Indian style. Many astrologers are familiar to use both the formats, but, some may not be comfortable to use a newer method in which they are not familiar. So we use both the charts in our books when we started bringing the English versions of our books for the benefit of every one. But there is a hitch here in the Jamakkol prasanam book. In the Jamakkol Aarudam technique, the Jama or the outer planets are marked outside the zodiac squares. It is easily written in the South Indian style of charts. But to accommodate the outer planets in the external corners of the North Indian charts it is a challenging one. We are working on this and will find a way out to this snag. In this present book we could use the South Indian charts only. We request the cooperation of our astrological friends.

South Indian style of horoscope chart

Guru		Mercury Venus	Sun Rahu
	Natal chart		Asc
Sat°			Mars Moon
Ketu			

This is the South Indian style horoscope chart with the Cancer Ascendant and the respective planetary positions.

North Indian style of the horoscope chart.

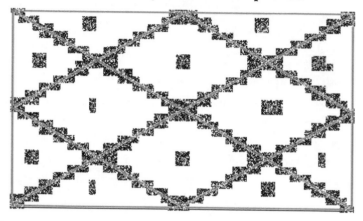

The main differences between the North Indian style of horoscope and the South Indian horoscope charts are as follows.

The rasis are fixed in the South Indian style of horoscope. In the South Indian charts, the lagna is put in the rasis wherever they are placed. Whereas the rasis are movable in the North Indian method of horoscope according to the Lagna / the Ascendant. Here, the ascendant is always marked in the top center square.

The South Indian horoscope is read in the clock wise direction and the North Indian horoscope is read in the anticlock wise direction. The ascendant can be marked in any square depending upon the horoscope in the South Indian style. Two small slanting lines are marked at the left corner of the square where the Ascendant is located in the South Indian chart. Usually the squares in the South Indian style are not numbered though the numbers are used to count the houses. The number 1 starts from the ascendant and runs continuously till the 12th house, but usually the numbers are not written inside the squares. In the North Indian charts, generally, the numbers from 1 to 12 are written in all the respective squares.

Appendix 3

Serial number	Rasi	English equivalent
1	Mesha	Aries
2	Rishabha	Taurus
3	Mithuna	Gemini
4	Kataka	Cancer
5	Simha	Leo
6	Kanya	Virgo
7	Thula	Libra
8	Virschika	Scorpio
9	Dhanus	Sagittarius
10	Makara	Capricorn
11	Kumbha	Aquarius
12	Meena	Pisces

Appendix 4

Serial number	Planets	English equivalents
1	Surya	Sun
2	Chandra	Moon
3	Chevvai	Mars
4	Bhudhan	Mercury
5	Guru	Jupiter
6	Sukra	Venus
7	Saturn	Saturn
8	Rahu	Dragon's head
9	Ketu	Dragon's tail

Appendix 5

In the second volume of Jamakkol prasanam some of the topics which are going to be discussed are:

1. Will I get a child?

2. What is the problem with my child?

3. Will the child be safe?

4. Can I go for an adopted child?

5. When will the baby be born?

6. Who is the father of this child?

7. When will my child speak?

8. What is my disease?

9. Will I get succeed in my mission?

10. What is my dream last night?

11. How much money I have in my hand now?

12. Can I undergo this surgery?

13. Will the missing person come back safe?

14. Where is my jewel?

15. Where is my document?

16. Where is my father?

17. When will get the letter from Canada?

18. When will I get the job?

19. Where can I install my bore well

20. In how many feet I will get water?

21. What is the quality of the water?

22. What is the quantity of the water?

23. Will I get water here?

24. Can you guess my question?

25. Will I be able to repay my debts?

26. Will I get success in exam/litigation/election?

27. Will the couple rejoin?

28. What is the cost of this car?

29. Am I affected by black magic?

30. How to identify death in the prasanam?

31. What is the object in my hand?

32. Which is my correct horoscope?

33. What is my birth star?

34. Will I go abroad?

35. Will I get the loan?

36. Is there any dosha in my family?

37. Will I get cured in this hospital?

38. Will the accident victim survive? Can we spend for him?

39. Will I get transfer /promotion?

40. Can I change my job?

41. Can I set an agricultural farm?

42. Will this servant be loyal to me?

43. Will I get divorce?

44. Will I repay my debts?

45. Will I get the approval letter?

46. Will I get my money back?

47. Is there a second marriage for me?

48. Can I do this job/business?

49. Can I buy this house/car/property?

50. Which God I can worship?

And many more.........

1. The various Jama graha arrangements show different results for the same query. Why?

2. What is the message from the exalted and the debilitated planets in the Jama graha?

3. If the outer planet and inner planet in a rasi are same, what is the significance?

4. Do the stars in which the outer planets locate have any implication?

5. How to determine the timing of events?

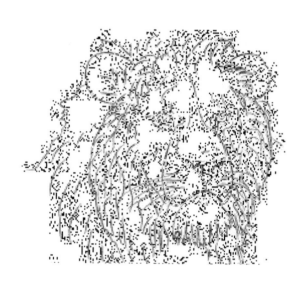

Made in the USA
Middletown, DE
05 July 2022